WHAT

To Do In

ARIZONA

Your Comprehensive Guide to Arizona:
Unveiling Hidden Treasures

Beverly Hilton

COPYRIGHT NOTICE

This publication is copyright protected. This is only for personal use. No part of this publication may be, including but not limited to, reproduced, in any form or medium, stored in a data retrieval system or transmitted by or through any means, without prior written permission from the Author / Publisher.

Legal action will be pursued if this is breached.

DISCLAIMER

Please note that the information contained within this document is for educational purposes only. The information contained herein has been obtained from sources believed to be reliable at the time of publication. The opinions expressed herein are subject to change without notice.

Readers acknowledge that the Author / Publisher is not engaging in rendering legal, financial or professional advice. The Publisher / Author disclaims all warranties as to the accuracy, completeness, or adequacy of such information.

The Publisher assumes no liability for errors, omissions, or inadequacies in the information contained herein or from the interpretations thereof. The publisher / Author specifically disclaims any liability from the use or application of the information contained herein or from the interpretations thereof.

TABLE OF CONTENTS

Copyright Notice 1
Disclaimer 3
TABLE OF CONTENTS 4
    INTRODUCTION 13

PURPOSE OF THIS BOOK 13
    Exploring Arizona's Diversity.. 14
    The Allure Of The Grand Canyon 16
    Embracing Tucson's Heritage 17
    Hidden Gems And Mistakes To Avoid 18
    CHAPTER 1 20

ESSENTIAL PREPARATIONS 20
    What You Should Know Before You Go 20
    Understanding Arizona's Climate 21
    Packing The Essentials... 22
    Researching Your Destinations 23
    Plan Your Itinerary 24
    Transportation Options 25

Staying Safe And Healthy 26
Cultural Sensitivity And Respect 27
CHAPTER 2 29

NAVIGATING THE LOCATION 29

Understanding Arizona's Geography And Climate 29
The Many Landscapes Of Arizona.. 30
The Climate Of Arizona 32
Navigating The Terrain 33
Understanding Local Flora And Fauna 35
Engaging With Local Communities 36
CHAPTER 3 39

PLANNING YOUR TRIP 39

Creating An Itinerary For The Perfect Visit 39
Understanding Your Travel Style... 40
Setting Your Duration 41
Researching Destinations 42
Creating A Balanced Itinerary 43
Packing For Your Adventure.. 45
Making Reservations 46
Embracing Flexibility 47
Engaging With Locals 47

Reflecting On Your Experience 48

CHAPTER 4 50

PHEONIX 50

What To Do And Not To Do In Arizona's Capital 50

Key Attractions 51

Getting Around Phoenix 54

Dining In Phoenix 56

Embracing The Desert Lifestyle 57

CHAPTER 5 60

SCOTTSDALE 60

What To Do And Not To Do In This Desert Oasis 60

Key Attractions 61

Getting Around Scottsdale 65

Dining In Scottsdale 66

Embracing The Scottsdale Vibe 67

CHAPTER 6 70

SEDONA 70

What To Do And Not Do In The Red Rocks 70

Key Attractions 71

Embracing The Sedona Experience 75

Connecting To Sedona's Spiritual Side 76

CHAPTER 7 80

FLAGSTAFF... 80
   What To Do And Not To Do In This Mountain Town 80
   Key Attractions 81
   Embracing Flagstaff's Unique Vibe 85
   Connecting With Nature 87
   CHAPTER 8 90

GRAND CANYON NATIONAL PARK 90
   What To Do And Not To Do At This Natural Wonder............ 90
   Key Attractions 91
   Embracing The Grand Canyon Experience............................ 96
   CHAPTER 9 99

TUCSON.. 99
   What To Do And Not To Do In The Old Pueblo..................... 99
   Key Attractions 100
   Embracing Tucson Culture And Cuisine 105
   CHAPTER 10 109

LAKE HAVASU CITY 109
   What To Do And Not To Do By The Water......................... 109
   Key Attractions 110

- Embracing Lake Havasu Lifestyle 114
- CHAPTER 11 118

YUMA 118
- What To Do And Not To Do In The Sunniest City 118
- Key Attractions 119
- Embracing Yuma Culture 123
- CHAPTER 12 127

PRESCOTT 127
- What To Do And Not To Do In Arizona's Mile High City 127
- Key Attractions 128
- Exploring Prescott's Culture 132
- CHAPTER 13 136

TOMBSTONE 136
- What To Do And Not To Do In The Town Too Tough To Die 136
- Key Attractions 137
- The Spirit Of Tombstone 141
- CHAPTER 14 145

PAYSON 145
- What To Do And Not To Do In The Heart Of Arizona 145

Key Attractions	146
The Spirit Of Payson	150
CHAPTER 15	153

BISBEE 153
What To Do And Not To Do In This Historic Mining Town	153
Key Attractions	154
The Spirit Of Bisbee	158
CHAPTER 16	161

APACHE JUNCTION 161
What To Do And Not To Do In The East Valley	161
Key Attractions	162
The Spirit Of Apache Junction	166
CHAPTER 17	169

JEROME 169
What To Do And Not To Do In Arizona's Ghost Town	169
Key Attractions	170
The Spirit Of Jerome	174
CHAPTER 18	178

SHOW LOW 178
What To Do And Not To Do In The White Mountains	178

Key Attractions 179
The Charm Of Show Low 183
CHAPTER 19 187

GLOBE 187

What To Do And Not To Do In The Heart Of The Copper Country 187
Key Attractions 188
The Heart Of Copper Country 192
CHAPTER 20 196

SAFETY TIPS FOR ARIZONA 196

Things To Avoid For A Safer Experience 196
Understanding The Environment 197
Wildlife Encounters 199
Vehicle Safety 202
Respecting Local Customs And Laws 203
CHAPTER 21 206

CULTURAL SENSITIVITY 206

What Not To Do When Interacting With Local Communities 206
Understanding Arizona's Diverse Culture 207
Respecting Traditions And Customs 209

Engaging With Local Economies 211
Interact With Indigenous Communities 212
CHAPTER 22 216

ENVIRONMENTAL CONSIDERATIONS 216
What To Do And Not To Do To Protect Arizona's Natural Beauty 216
Understanding Arizona's Environment 217
Water Conservation 219
Wildlife Protection 220
Fire Safety 222
Sustainable Practices 223
CHAPTER 23 226

DINING DO'S AND DON'TS 226
What To Do And Not To Do In Arizona's Culinary Scene 226
Embracing Local Flavors 227
Understanding Etiquette 229
Exploring Food Festivals 230
Exploring Ethnic Cuisine 232
Experience Wine And Spirits 234
CHAPTER 24 237

DEPARTURE TIPS 237

What To Remember Before Leaving Arizona 237
Take Time For Reflection 238
Souvenirs And Mementos 239
Stay Connected 241
Final Exploration 243
Preparing For The Journey Home 244

INTRODUCTION

PURPOSE OF THIS BOOK

When I first arrived in Arizona, I was instantly fascinated. The panorama spread like a brilliant painting, with huge deserts, towering red cliffs, and magnificent mountains. Every curve and turn on the twisting roads seemed to foreshadow an adventure waiting to happen. Arizona is a state that lives on contrast—one moment you're surrounded by the vast, parched Sonoran Desert, the next you're gazing up at the snow-capped peaks of the San Francisco Mountains. Each location has its own distinct appeal, but within all of this beauty, I discovered that some encounters may quickly change from memorable to terrible if you're not careful.

That's why I decided to write this book, "What Not to Do in Arizona." It's about more than just avoiding typical hazards; it's about enriching your adventure and making sure you enjoy every moment. As a traveler who has visited many of Arizona's nooks and crannies, I would want to share what I've learned. Trust me, navigating this engrossing condition may be as difficult as it is rewarding, especially if you don't know what to look out for.

This guide contains great insights and practical recommendations to make your trip unique. Whether you're planning your first trip or returning to familiar places, I want you to enter Arizona with confidence and excitement. The goal of this book is to emphasize both the dazzling attractions and the potential pitfalls that can turn a vacation into a disaster.

Exploring Arizona's Diversity

Allow me to walk you through the numerous elements of Arizona. Imagine you've arrived in Phoenix, the state's busy capital. It's a city that combines modernity and history, with sleek skyscrapers coexisting with historical sites. The mornings are bathed in golden sunlight, and the nights bring a chilly wind that speaks of adventure. However, while it is tempting to get right into the city's lively culture, there are a few places and habits to avoid. I remember my first night out— what a mistake it was to ignore the local suggestions! Instead of dining on authentic Southwest cuisine, I found myself in a chain restaurant that could have been anywhere in the country. Lesson learned: get local guidance!

As I journeyed north, I arrived in Sedona, which feels like a spiritual oasis. The red rocks stand tall against the azure sky, their brilliant colors altering as the sun moves across the sky. Hiking the trails here is nothing short of beautiful, but I soon realized that not all paths are created equal. One sunny afternoon, I headed out on a popular path without considering the conditions or my own capabilities, only to find myself suffering through a more difficult course than I had anticipated. If you're planning a hike in Sedona, follow trail advisories and be aware of your physical limitations; the views are spectacular, but safety should always come first.

I was drawn to Flagstaff because of its high elevation and the close splendor of the San Francisco Peaks. The historic downtown area is bustling with coffee shops and artisanal retailers. It's an ideal location to relax with a nice drink and take in the local atmosphere. However, as I toured the area, I became dissatisfied with the parking possibilities. Many visitors overlook this critical element, resulting in wasted time hunting for parking in congested places. If you want to explore Flagstaff, take public transit or arrive early to secure a nice parking spot.

The Allure Of The Grand Canyon

Ah, the Grand Canyon—words cannot express its grandeur. I distinctly recall standing at the brink, peering into the abyss, feeling both humbled and exhilarated. The immensity was nearly overwhelming, and the canyon walls changed colors from orange, crimson, and purple as the sun sunk below the horizon. Despite its spectacular beauty, the Grand Canyon contains its fair share of tourist traps. One of the biggest mistakes I made during my vacation was giving in to the allure of the pricey souvenir shops that line the park. While it's nice to have a souvenir, I discovered that shopping with local artists outside the park offers considerably more unique and meaningful items.

As I progressed deeper down the canyon, I made another mistake. I chose to take on a trail that was way beyond my comfort level without appropriate preparation. The rough terrain, sudden elevation changes, and persistent sun made for a tough encounter. It taught me the importance of being informed—check trail ratings and bring plenty of water. The canyon's beauty demands respect, so make sure to prepare appropriately.

Embracing Tucson's Heritage

Tucson was another highlight of my Arizona vacation, with its rich cultural past. The combination of Native American, Mexican, and Western influences results in a vivid tapestry that can be seen in the architecture, cuisine, and art. I spent time at the Arizona-Sonora Desert Museum learning about the desert's flora and fauna. But oh, how I wished I had escaped the sweltering afternoon heat! The sun shone down fiercely, and I frantically sought shade. If you visit Tucson, arrange your activities early in the morning or late in the afternoon to avoid the scorching heat.

Another important recommendation is the local gastronomic scene. Tucson is a UNESCO City of Gastronomy, thus the cuisine is exceptional. However, I learnt the hard way that not all restaurants are equal. I found up in a chain diner instead of enjoying traditional Sonoran hot dogs. Research local restaurants, ask for advice, and don't be afraid to try food trucks; you'll be astonished by the variety of cuisines available.

Hidden Gems And Mistakes To Avoid

My trek through Arizona has taken me to some hidden gems—places that often go overlooked but are well worth the time. Bisbee is one such treasure, a historic mining town with a peculiar charm that captivated me. Its colorful buildings, tiny winding alleyways, and artistic attitude create a friendly and exciting environment. But be warned: the town is hilly! I made the mistake of wearing sandals instead of sturdy shoes and ended up regretting it halfway up a steep street. A nice pair of walking shoes can significantly improve your experience.

Similarly, Jerome, a ghost town nestled on a hillside, sparked my imagination. The town's rich history and artistic community are intriguing, although it may be overly touristy. I observed that several businesses sell costly souvenirs that do not accurately depict Jerome's personality. Instead, visit local galleries and support artists that actually embody the spirit of our unique community.

Conclusion: As I reflect on my travels around Arizona, I understand that this state is more than just a destination; it is an adventure waiting to happen. Each city and site provides its own set of wonders and lessons. It's a location where the landscapes tell stories, where every road journey is an adventure, and the air smells of sagebrush and possibilities.

I hope this book helps you on your adventure around Arizona. By sharing what I've learned—both the good and the bad—I hope to help you traverse this amazing state with ease and confidence. From critical preparations and terrain navigation to vibrant cities and magnificent vistas, each chapter will provide you all the information you need to make the most of your time in Arizona.

So, whether you're planning your first vacation or returning to see familiar locations, keep in mind that the best adventures are often seasoned with wisdom. Let us go on this trip together, making every moment in Arizona a memorable experience. Welcome to the wonders of Arizona—let's explore them together!

CHAPTER 1

ESSENTIAL PREPARATIONS

What You Should Know Before You Go

As I planned my experiences in Arizona, I understood that the details are crucial to a good trip. The state is a beautiful patchwork of landscapes, cultures, and activities, and traversing it demands some foresight and preparation. I've discovered that a few easy preparations can dramatically improve your experience, changing a routine visit into an unforgettable excursion. So, allow me to share the critical preparations that made my trip in Arizona not just delightful, but truly unforgettable.

Understanding Arizona's Climate

First and foremost, you need to comprehend Arizona's climate. I recall stepping off the plane in Phoenix and being surrounded by a surge of heat that felt like I had walked into an oven. The warm embrace of the desert sun is one thing, but the summer heat can be exhausting. Temperatures can go considerably beyond 100°F (38°C), particularly in cities such as Phoenix and Tucson. In contrast, winter temperatures can drop below freezing in northern places such as Flagstaff, blanketing the area in snow.

So, what have I done? I checked the weather prediction for each destination I planned to visit. Layering was my secret weapon. I selected light, breathable clothing for the warmer climates, but I also brought warmer layers for my journey north. As I frequently state, "In Arizona, it's always wise to prepare for a weather whiplash!""

Packing The Essentials

Now that you've understood the weather, let's speak about packing. While it may be tempting to overpack, I discovered the hard way that a well-curated luggage is significantly more useful. Here are the essentials that I recommend:

Comfortable Footwear: Arizona is a hiker's dream, so whether you're traversing the city streets of Phoenix or hiking through the trails of Sedona, you'll need a reliable pair of shoes. I purchased an excellent pair of hiking boots, but I also packed comfy sandals for relaxing after long days of exploring.

Sun Protection: The desert sun can be harsh. I cannot emphasize enough how important sunscreen, sunglasses, and wide-brimmed hats are. After one afternoon in Sedona without sufficient sunblock, I learnt this lesson the hard way. I ended up with a sunburn, which ruined my enjoyment of the breathtaking red rock scenery.

Hydration Equipment: Water is your best buddy in Arizona. The arid atmosphere can quickly cause dehydration, particularly during outdoor activity. I always carried a refillable water bottle; if you plan on hiking for an extended period of time, consider a hydration pack. It's a minor issue, but staying hydrated made my hikes significantly more enjoyable.

First-Aid Kit: Accidents happen, especially while you're out and about. Bring a first-aid kit. I always travel with a simple first-aid pack that includes bandages, antiseptic wipes, and any personal meds. It's pleasant to know that I'm prepared for tiny mishaps.

Camera And Journal: Arizona is breathtaking, and I wanted to document every moment. I always travel with a camera to capture the breathtaking scenery and vivid sunsets. I also kept a journal to record my experiences and ideas; you never know when a recollection can become a cherished narrative.

Researching Your Destinations

Before embarking on my tour, I spent time researching each site I planned to visit. Arizona is huge, with attractions as diverse as its scenery. Understanding each place's history, culture, and distinct attractions made my travels much more meaningful.

For example, I was eager to hear about the indigenous civilizations that molded Arizona long before the state was established. In cities like Tucson and Flagstaff, I visited local museums and cultural institutions to obtain a better understanding of the land and its history. I also learned about the Saguaro cactus, which is an iconic symbol of the Sonoran Desert. Knowing the tales behind these locations provided depth to my trip.

Plan Your Itinerary

Creating a well-planned itinerary was one of the most enjoyable portions of my preparations. I tried to divide my time between iconic sights and hidden gems, ensuring that I saw the best of Arizona. Here are some tips that I found useful:

Must-See Attractions: I compiled a list of must-see destinations, including the Grand Canyon, Sedona's red rocks, and Phoenix's dynamic downtown area. Prioritizing these prominent destinations gave me enough time to explore.

Hidden Gems: In addition to the major attractions, I've added lesser-known locations that I discovered while researching. For example, I discovered the delightful small town of Bisbee, which has eclectic art galleries and a rich mining heritage. These unexpected gems frequently become the highlights of my journey.

Flexible Scheduling: I had a rough plan for each day, but I left room for improvisation. Some of my most memorable moments occurred when I took a detour or remained longer at a particularly picturesque location. Be willing to change your plans; Arizona has a way of surprising you.

Local Activities And Festivals: Prior to my vacation, I examined local calendars to see what activities were scheduled for my stay. I was fortunate to stumble onto the Tucson Gem & Mineral Show, which highlighted the region's abundant geological resources. Attending local events can provide a distinct perspective on the culture and community.

Transportation Options

As I planned my trip, I considered how to explore Arizona efficiently. While I enjoy the flexibility of driving, I quickly realized that some locations are best explored using specific transportation options:

Renting An Automobile: I needed an automobile for my journey. Arizona's attractions are spaced out, and being able to explore at my own leisure felt liberating. I made cautious to reserve my rental car in advance, especially during peak tourist seasons. A dependable vehicle enabled me to venture off the beaten road and explore hidden gems.

Public Transportation: In places such as Phoenix and Tucson, public transportation is an alternative. In Phoenix, I used the Valley Metro Light Rail to go around, which was both convenient and inexpensive. If you don't want to drive, you should look into local public transportation choices.

Tours And Guided Experiences: I occasionally chose guided tours, particularly while visiting historically significant sites such as the ancient cliff dwellings at Montezuma Castle National Monument. Local guides provided information that I may have ignored on my own. Furthermore, it alleviated the stress of traversing unknown terrain.

Staying Safe And Healthy

Health and safety should always be a top priority, especially in a state with such different topography and weather. Here are some techniques I used to safeguard my safety during my travels:

Stay Informed: I kept myself informed about the present conditions in the areas I planned to visit. For example, certain hiking routes may close due to inclement weather or repair, thus checking official websites or local visitor centers was essential.

Wildlife Awareness: Arizona is home to a variety of wildlife, including snakes and scorpions. I learned to be cautious while hiking and to stick to indicated trails. Respecting nature leads to a safe and happy experience.

Emergency Contacts: I stored key phone numbers for local emergency agencies and hospitals. Having this information at my fingertips gave me peace of mind.

Cultural Sensitivity And Respect

As I journeyed around Arizona, I became more aware of the value of cultural awareness. The state is home to various Native American tribes, each with their own customs and traditions. Here's how I handled my interactions respectfully:

Learn About Local Cultures: Before visiting Native American reservations or cultural sites, I spent time learning about the tribes' practices and histories. Understanding their significance enhanced my admiration for the area.

Ask Before Photographing: When touring religious sites, I was cautious about snapping pictures. I always asked for permission before capturing a moment. This little act of respect goes a long way toward preserving local traditions.

Support Local Artisans: Rather than buying mass-produced souvenirs, I looked for local artisans and craftsmen. This not only benefits the neighborhood, but it also broadens my experience with true gems.

Final Thoughts: As I wrap off this chapter on critical preparations, I hope you feel ready and encouraged to go on your own journey through Arizona. Arizona has something for everyone, from its breathtaking landscapes to its rich culture and different experiences. The key to making the most of it is to plan ahead of time and be willing to learn new things.

Accept the adventure that awaiting you. Know the weather, pack intelligently, immerse yourself in local culture, and be open to surprises. Arizona is a land of wonders, and with the appropriate planning, your trip may be a stunning tapestry of memories and experiences.

So, let us hit the road! The vast skies of Arizona are calling, and believe me, you are in for a spectacular ride

CHAPTER 2

NAVIGATING THE LOCATION

Understanding Arizona's Geography And Climate

As I stood on the rim of the Grand Canyon, staring out over the wide, layered expanse of red rock stretching as far as the eye could see, I couldn't help but be amazed by Arizona's geographical diversity. This state is a region of opposites, where parched deserts give way to lush pine forests and towering mountains, and vibrant cities vibrate with activity amidst the silence of nature. Understanding Arizona's geography and climate is critical for any traveler wishing to explore this gorgeous country, and I'm delighted to share my observations from my own experiences.

The Many Landscapes Of Arizona

One of the first things I noticed as I traveled across Arizona was the beautiful variety of landscapes. I felt the state's energy from the time I landed in Phoenix, a big city surrounded by mountains.

Deserts: As I traveled south to Tucson, the Sonoran Desert surrounded me with its own splendor. The renowned Saguaro cactus looms tall, its spindly limbs arching aloft. I took a time to appreciate the desert's subtleties: the vivid wildflowers that bloom in the spring, the diverse animal life that inhabits this hard environment, and the breathtaking sunsets that paint the sky pink and orange. I discovered that the greatest way to explore the desert is on foot. Trails like those in Saguaro National Park uncovered hidden gems and provided a closer look at this distinct ecology.

Mountains And Forests: Heading north, I arrived in Flagstaff, tucked among the Ponderosa pines. The height here (almost 7,000 feet) was a welcome respite from the scorching heat I had become accustomed to. I could feel the temperature dropping as I explored the Coconino National Forest. Hiking the trails, I was surrounded by the aroma of pine and the sound of rustling leaves. The chilly, clean air lifted my spirits. This was an unexpected side of Arizona, and it rapidly became one of my favorite escapes.

Canyons And Plateaus: No trip to Arizona is complete without visiting the Grand Canyon. Standing on the South Rim, I was in awe of the vast abyss formed by the Colorado River over millions of years. The canyon walls' vivid colors changed with the sun, revealing a palette that appeared almost unearthly. I chose to take a guided tour, which allowed me to learn about the geology and history of this natural beauty. The guide's stories about the ancient Puebloan peoples deepened my comprehension of the country and its significance.

High Desert And Valleys: Then there's the high desert, which includes Sedona. The breathtaking red rock formations create a dramatic scene that appears to pulse with electricity. I enjoyed hiking around Cathedral Rock and Bell Rock, where the red sandstone gleamed in the late afternoon sunlight. I learned about the local vortex locations, which are supposed to be energy hubs. While I was skeptical about the theory, I couldn't ignore the sense of peace that came over me when I meditated at one of these spots.

The Climate Of Arizona

Now, let's talk about the weather, which determines everything from what to wear to when to visit certain places.

Desert Climate: In the southern regions, such as Phoenix and Tucson, the climate is defined by desert characteristics. Summers may be quite hot, with temperatures frequently exceeding 100°F (38°C). I immediately discovered that the best times to visit these regions are in the early morning or late afternoon, when the heat is more bearable. During my visit in late spring, I enjoyed the flowering wildflowers that decorated the desert floor, providing a welcome contrast to the parched scenery. I also made an effort to stay hydrated, constantly carrying a water bottle and taking frequent rests in the shade.

Mountain Climate: As I headed north into Flagstaff, the weather changed considerably. The temps here were lower, and I found myself grabbing for sweaters and jackets, particularly in the nights. The high desert has four distinct seasons, with winter providing a lovely blanket of snow. I recall strolling around downtown Flagstaff during the winter holiday season, the streets lit up with glittering lights and the scent of fresh pine in the air. Despite the chill, it seemed like a snug mountain town: friendly and warm.

Monsoon Season: Another notable characteristic of Arizona's climate is the monsoon season, which lasts from June to September. During this period, thunderstorms might arrive unexpectedly, bringing torrential rain and amazing lighting displays. During my visit to Tucson, I had firsthand experience with this. I had been hiking late in the afternoon when heavy clouds loomed ominously. Suddenly, the heavens opened, and I was caught in a rainstorm. While it was initially unsettling, I quickly came to appreciate the rain's cooling effect after a hot day. The desert appeared to come alive with bright colors following the storm, making the trip worthwhile.

Navigating The Terrain

With Arizona's diverse landscape and fluctuating climate, navigating the terrain requires some planning and knowledge.

Driving In Arizona: I discovered that renting a car was the most effective way to explore the state. The roadways are well-maintained, and traveling along the gorgeous vistas is a unique experience in itself. I did a road trip from Phoenix to Sedona, and the scenery was spectacular. The red rocks of Sedona became visible, soaring dramatically against the pure blue sky. I strongly advise you to keep your camera handy; there will be numerous opportunities for unexpected photo stops. Just keep in mind the distances between destinations; Arizona is much larger than it appears, so plan your journey ahead of time.

Hiking Trails: Arizona is famous for its hiking trails, which range from pleasant strolls to strenuous climbs. Before tackling the trails, I always checked the trail conditions and difficulty ratings. Websites like All Trails became my go-to resources for determining the finest treks for my skill level. One noteworthy hike was the West Fork Trail in Oak Creek Canyon. The shaded trail meandered alongside a gurgling creek, and I felt a sense of calm wash over me as I hiked. The luxuriant foliage felt like a hidden realm among the red cliffs.

Respecting Nature: As I explored Arizona's wild spaces, I realized how important it is to respect the ecosystem. I always observed the Leave No Trace rules, leaving the trails as pristine as I found them. This entailed packing out all of my rubbish, staying on designated trails, and avoiding disturbing the wildlife. During one hike, I saw a family of deer feeding quietly. Watching them in their native surroundings served as a reminder of the ecosystem's beauty and fragility.

Understanding Local Flora And Fauna

Arizona's diverse biodiversity is another intriguing facet of its landscape. The state contains a wide range of ecosystems, each with its own set of flora and animals.

Desert Life: The flora and fauna of the Sonoran Desert impressed me with their persistence. The Saguaro cactus, with its towering height, can live for more than 150 years. I went on a guided tour of the Desert Botanical Garden in Phoenix, where I learnt about the different types of cactus and succulents that thrive in this harsh environment. I marveled at how life thrived in such arid settings, demonstrating nature's tremendous resilience.

Mountain Ecosystems: As I climbed into the forests of Flagstaff, the environment changed radically. The thick pines and cool temps provided a safe haven for wildlife, including elk and other bird species. I spent the afternoon birdwatching, using a handbook to identify the various avian species. The birds' brilliant colors against the green backdrop were stunning, and I felt a connection to the natural world that left me feeling reenergized.

Conservation Efforts: I also learnt about Arizona's conservation efforts, which strive to maintain its unique ecosystems. Visiting the Arizona-Sonora Desert Museum allowed me to witness firsthand the dedication to preserving indigenous species. I was very impressed by their work with endangered species such as the desert tortoise. Understanding the problems these animals face has increased my appreciation for Arizona's delicate balance of life.

Engaging With Local Communities

Finally, comprehending Arizona's topography and climate requires interaction with the varied groups that call this state home.

Cultural Richness: As I explored urban places such as Tucson and Phoenix, I was amazed by the complex cultural tapestry created by Native American, Hispanic, and Western influences. Attending local festivals and events helped me to fully immerse myself in this vibrant culture. I clearly recall the Tucson Meet Yourself festival, when I sampled traditional music, dance, and delectable cuisine from diverse cultural origins.

Indigenous Communities: Visiting indigenous villages was another pleasure of my trip. I had the opportunity to see the Hopi reservation and learn about their customs and way of life. The warmth I experienced was remarkable, and the elders' stories touched me deeply. They underlined their connection to the land and the need to preserve their culture for future generations.

Supporting Local Companies: Throughout my journey, I made a concerted effort to support local companies. Whether dining at family-owned restaurants or purchasing handcrafted items from local craftsmen, I discovered that this not only enhanced my experience but also benefited the communities I visited.

Final Thoughts: As I ponder on my trip across Arizona, I am constantly astounded by the state's breathtaking terrain and climate. From the sun-kissed deserts to the towering mountains, every region of Arizona has a distinct experience waiting to be found. Understanding this diversified terrain has helped me appreciate the state's natural beauty and cultural complexity.

To navigate Arizona, you must be both prepared and willing to explore. Respecting the earth, engaging with local populations, and enjoying the range of activities available made my travels significantly more rewarding. As I packed my things for the next stage of my journey, I knew Arizona will always retain a special place in my heart as a land of beauty, tenacity, and wonderful memories.

So, as you go on your own adventure through Arizona, remember to take your time, enjoy the views, and allow the charm of this magnificent state to surround you. Whether you're trekking through a canyon or sipping locally made coffee at a quaint café, Arizona's wonders will make an indelible impression on your soul.

CHAPTER 3

PLANNING YOUR TRIP

Creating An Itinerary For The Perfect Visit

As I sat at a quaint café in downtown Phoenix, the smells of fresh coffee mingled with the sounds of lively conversations around me, I felt a surge of anticipation rise within me. I was planning an itinerary for my impending trip to Arizona, a place I had grown to admire for its magnificent scenery and rich cultural legacy. Planning is essential, especially in a place as diverse and large as Arizona. My experiences have taught me that a well-planned itinerary can mean the difference between a chaotic trip and a memorable one. Allow me to offer my views on how to plan the ideal itinerary for your Arizona trip.

Understanding Your Travel Style

The first step in arranging any trip is to identify your travel style. Are you an adventurous soul looking to walk through canyons and explore tough paths, or do you prefer a more relaxing pace, soaking up local culture and taking leisurely strolls through picturesque towns? Personally, I fall somewhere in the middle—I enjoy the excitement of outdoor experiences while still appreciating the ability to relax and interact with local communities.

Adventurous Itineraries: If you're looking for excitement, consider devoting a large chunk of your vacation to national parks and outdoor activities. The Grand Canyon, Sedona, and Saguaro National Park all offer spectacular routes and chances for exploration. I recall my own journey to the Grand Canyon, when I ascended the Bright Angel Trail, delving into the canyon's depths and marveling at the shifting sceneries with each step. Make careful to schedule time for both short hikes and longer journeys to truly appreciate the park's beauty.

Cultural Experiences: For individuals who enjoy cultural immersion, I recommend visiting museums, art galleries, and historical places. The Heard Museum in Phoenix is a treasure mine of Native American art and culture, offering a thorough grasp of the region's background. I was enthralled by the storytelling woven throughout the displays, making it an ideal stop for anybody interested in Arizona's cultural tapestry.

Setting Your Duration

Next, determine how long you can stay in Arizona. The optimal time varies greatly depending on your interests, but I recommend at least five to seven days to really enjoy the state's beauty and diversity.

Short Getaways: If you only have a few days, focus on one region. For example, you may spend three days touring Sedona's famed red rock formations, sampling local cuisine, and taking in the bustling art scene. A visit to Slide Rock State Park for a refreshing soak in natural waters could be a fun highlight.

Extended Adventures: For those with additional time, I recommend a loop that combines urban activities and natural beauties. A ten-day itinerary may begin in Phoenix, travel via Sedona, the Grand Canyon, and conclude in Flagstaff. This way, you'll get to enjoy the best of both worlds: metropolitan bustling and tranquil countryside.

Researching Destinations

With a better understanding of your travel style and duration, it's time to start researching. Arizona has numerous attractions, each of which provides unique experiences that reflect the state's identity.

Top Attractions: Start by listing the must-see attractions. My personal favorites are:

Grand Canyon National Park: Visit Grand Canyon National Park for breathtaking views that make any journey to Arizona worthwhile. Plan to spend at least a full day exploring the South Rim and taking in the magnificent views.

Sedona's Red Rocks: Sedona's Red Rocks offer breathtaking scenery for outdoor activities such as hiking and bicycling. Don't miss the Chapel of the Holy Cross, whose architectural splendor merges in with the surroundings.

Tucson's Mission San Xavier Del Bac: Visit Tucson's Mission San Xavier del Bac, a historic Spanish mission with stunning architecture and a rich history of Arizona.

Hidden Jewels: While well-known attractions are absolutely worthwhile, I recommend that you seek out hidden jewels as well. The Ghost Town of Jerome, built on a mountainside, provides a unique peek into Arizona's mining past as well as breathtaking vistas of the Verde Valley. I enjoyed browsing around the tiny stores, looking for unusual items, and learning about the town's rich history.

Creating A Balanced Itinerary

With your list of sights and attractions, it's time to plan a well-balanced itinerary. I've discovered that variety is the key to a successful trip—balancing action with leisure, nature and culture, and sightseeing with downtime.

Sample Itinerary: Here's an example itinerary I created for a weeklong trip:

Day One: Arrive in Phoenix. Spend the afternoon seeing the Desert Botanical Garden and eating dinner at a nearby restaurant. Do not forget to sample the Sonoran hot dog!

Day Two: Travel to Sedona. Begin with a morning hike to Cathedral Rock, followed by lunch at a café with a view. In the afternoon, explore art galleries and watch the sunset from Airport Mesa.

Day Three: Explore Sedona with a jeep tour or visit Tlaquepaque Arts and Shopping Village.

Day Four: Drive to the Grand Canyon. Spend the day exploring the South Rim, stopping at several overlooks. Stay until sunset to see the canyon glow in shades of orange and crimson.

Day Five: Explore the area's geology and history by hiking the Bright Angel Trail or joining a guided tour. In the evening, you can camp under the stars or stay in one of the lodges.

Day Six: Travel to Flagstaff. Explore the city's breweries and enjoy a leisurely stroll through downtown. Visit the Lowell Observatory in the evening to gaze at the stars.

Day Seven: On Day seven, try visiting Walnut Canyon National Monument to observe old cliff dwellings or driving through Oak Creek Canyon.

Packing For Your Adventure

Now that you've planned your agenda, it's time to consider packing. Arizona's diverse environment requires you to be prepared for anything, from searing heat to frigid mountain nights.

Clothing Essentials: I always advocate layering. In the desert, temperatures can vary considerably between day and night. I brought light clothing, a warm fleece, and sturdy hiking boots. I also took a wide-brimmed hat and sunglasses to shield myself from the scorching sun.

Outdoor Gear: If you plan to hike or spend time outside, remember to bring a reusable water bottle, sunscreen, and a daypack. I learned the hard way that staying hydrated is essential in the Arizona heat, especially during vigorous activity. Having a portable charger for my phone was also a lifesaver, allowing me to photograph all of the breathtaking sights without fear of running out of battery.

Cultural Considerations: When visiting indigenous villages or sacred locations, please be respectful. I always look for any standards regarding suitable clothes and behavior. A short web search will help you navigate any cultural sensitivities.

Making Reservations

As my vacation approached, I made sure to make bookings, particularly for lodging and any tours or activities I intended to do.

Lodging Alternatives: Arizona has a wide selection of lodging alternatives, from luxurious resorts to lovely bed-and-breakfasts. I appreciated staying at a locally owned inn in Sedona, where the proprietors shared their favorite hiking trails and food ideas. Booking early is recommended, especially during peak tourist seasons.

Activity Reservations: For popular activities like guided tours of the Grand Canyon or hot air balloon rides in Phoenix, I found it helpful to book in advance. These experiences fill up quickly, so making a reservation insured that I didn't miss out on something I was looking forward to.

Embracing Flexibility

While a well-planned itinerary is necessary, I've learned that flexibility is also essential. Unexpected discoveries can lead to some of the most memorable memories.

Spontaneous Adventures: During my visit to Sedona, I discovered a local art festival that was not on my schedule. I spent the afternoon browsing unusual goods and conversing with the artists, taking in the bright environment. Allowing for spontaneity made my journey feel richer and more rewarding.

Weather Considerations: Arizona's weather can be unpredictable, particularly during the monsoon season. If rain disrupts your plans, consider visiting a local museum or taking a scenic drive through the rain-soaked landscape—the vistas can be even more breathtaking after a storm.

Engaging With Locals

One of the most enjoyable aspects of travel is the chance to interact with locals. I made it a point to interact with people wherever I went, whether it was conversing with shopkeepers, asking park rangers for recommendations, or attending local activities.

Local Tips: I noticed that locals typically have the best insider knowledge on hidden treasures and lesser-known attractions. During my stay in Tucson, I met a kind barista who recommended a favorite hiking trail away from the tourists, which led to a quiet waterfall that felt like a private paradise.

Cultural Experiences: Attending local events like farmers' markets and cultural festivals helped me gain a better knowledge of Arizona's rich legacy. I appreciated trying local cuisine and learning about the region's cultural practices.

Reflecting On Your Experience

As I finished my trip and thought on my experiences, I recognized that careful planning had enhanced my tour, allowing me to see the most that Arizona has to offer. Each day unfolded with purpose, and every moment felt deliberate, whether we were seeing breathtaking vistas or tasting the delicacies of the local cuisine.

Essentially, planning an itinerary for your trip to Arizona includes more than just filling your days with activities. It's about choosing experiences that speak to you, connecting with the place and its people, and creating memories that will last a lifetime. So, as you begin on your vacation, take the time to create a plan that matches your interests while allowing for spontaneity and connection. Arizona is ready to share its delights with you, and I am confident that your adventure will be as beautiful as mine was.

CHAPTER 4

PHEONIX

What To Do And Not To Do In Arizona's Capital

When I first arrived in Phoenix, I was immediately struck by the city's bright energy. The sun shone a golden light across the vast desert landscape, revealing the spectacular mountains that outline the skyline. Phoenix, Arizona's capital, is a thriving metropolis that blends urban sophistication with the wild beauty of the desert. Phoenix, with its rich culture, kind friendliness, and breathtaking natural surroundings, provides endless opportunities for discovery. However, there are some mistakes to avoid if you want to make the most of your trip. Allow me to give my tips on what to do and what not to do while seeing this vibrant city.

Key Attractions

The Desert Botanical Garden and the Phoenix Zoo are two of Phoenix's most recognizable attractions, and I found them both very captivating. Both areas provide a unique peek into the region's natural splendor and are ideal starting points for anybody wishing to explore Arizona's stunning terrain.

Desert Botanical Garden: My first destination on my Phoenix tour was the Desert Botanical Garden, a lovely haven of plants that exhibits the Sonoran Desert's magnificence. As I went through the garden's twisting paths, I was captivated by the vibrant colors and textures of the cactus, succulents, and indigenous plants.

What To Do

Explore The Trails: I walked through the 140-acre garden and found over 50,000 plants. Each portion of the garden tells a tale, with collections themed after distinct desert habitats. I especially appreciated the "Desert Discovery Loop," which taught me about the remarkable characteristics of desert flora. Bring your camera; there are many photo opportunities here.

Attend A Special Event: The garden frequently holds art exhibits and seasonal festivities. I was fortunate enough to attend an evening event where the garden was lit up with amazing light installations, creating a magical mood as the sun set over the desert.

Visit The Gift Shop: Visit the garden's gift shop for unusual gifts such as local artwork and desert horticulture literature. I found a lovely handcrafted ceramic pot, which now proudly hangs on my balcony as a remembrance of my stay in Phoenix.

What Not To Do

Don't Rush Your Visit: This is not a quick stop. Take your time and enjoy the views and sounds of the desert. I made the mistake of attempting to observe everything too quickly during my first visit, and I later discovered that I had missed the subtleties that make this garden so unique.

Avoid Visiting During Peak Heat: Avoid peak heat by visiting early in the morning or late afternoon, especially during summer months. I learnt this the hard way, and I spent an especially hot afternoon wishing I had planned better.

Phoenix Zoo: Just a short drive from the Desert Botanical Garden, I arrived at the Phoenix Zoo, one of the largest non-profit zoos in the United States. This 125-acre park is home to over 3,000 creatures from more than 400 species.

What To Do

Explore The Exhibits: The zoo's specialized zones offer unique experiences. The "Africa Trail" with African lions, cheetahs, and giraffes was a highlight for me. It was a magnificent opportunity to see the giraffes eat leaves from only a few feet away.

Participate In Animal Encounters: Get up close and personal with the zoo's residents. I had a fantastic experience feeding the giraffes and learning about their care and routines from the experienced zookeepers.

Take A Tram Ride: Take a tram ride to get a new perspective of the zoo. It is a peaceful approach to see the exhibits while resting your feet. I appreciated the cold breeze while riding through the diverse animal habitats.

What Not To Do

Don't Skip The Educational Programs: The zoo provides instructive activities and presentations throughout the day. Don't miss them. I made a point of attending a couple, and I came away with a renewed appreciation for wildlife conservation initiatives. Missing these would mean passing up an opportunity to learn more about the creatures and their environments.

Avoid Feeding Animals: Although animal encounters are enjoyable, feeding animals outside authorized places is strictly prohibited. It is critical to respect animals and their dietary demands. I watched someone attempting to feed a squirrel and instantly realized that such actions could be detrimental.

Getting Around Phoenix

As I made my way across the city, I learned that Phoenix is extremely spread out, so having a plan for moving around is critical.

What To Do

Rent A Car: Renting a car was the most convenient alternative, allowing me to explore at my own pace. The roads are generally easy to handle, and I enjoyed taking picturesque drives, particularly through Camelback Mountain.

Use Rideshare Services: Use rideshare services such as Uber and Lyft to avoid parking hassles and travel short distances. They are readily available and can be a convenient way to travel about the city.

What Not To Do

Don't Rely Solely On Public Transportation: Although Phoenix has a bus and light rail system, its availability may be limited in some regions. I initially attempted to rely on public transportation, which resulted in long waits and missed connections. If you're short on time, consider alternative modes of transportation.

Avoid Driving During Rush Hour: Avoid driving during rush hour as traffic can be crowded, particularly near downtown and main highways. I made a mental note to organize my trips outside of these hours in order to enjoy more comfortable rides.

Dining In Phoenix

The meal was without a doubt one of the highlights of my visit to Phoenix. The city has a strong food sector that reflects its various cultural influences.

What To Do

Try Local Cuisine: I tried local cuisine, especially Sonoran-style Mexican food. Tacos, tamales, and chimichangas became constants in my dining experience. One of my favorite restaurants was Los Dos Molinos, where I had a dish of smothered enchiladas with just the perfect kick.

Explore Food Markets: Explore food markets, including the popular Phoenix Public Market. I enjoyed browsing the vendors and tasting fresh veggies, artisan cheeses, and locally baked pastries. I ended up purchasing a few items to enjoy back at my hotel, elevating an average supper to a wonderful occasion.

What Not To Do

Don't Skip Breakfast: In Phoenix, breakfast is a must-have. The neighborhood breakfast establishments serve delectable dishes ranging from huevos rancheros to sumptuous pancakes. I recommend that you visit Snooze, an A.M. Eatery for a fantastic start to the day.

Avoid Chain Restaurants: While familiar chains are easily accessible, I recommend seeking out local restaurants. My most memorable dinners were at tiny, family-owned eateries that provided real cuisine and a welcoming ambiance.

Embracing The Desert Lifestyle

One of the most essential lessons I learned from my time in Phoenix was the value of embracing the desert lifestyle. The scenery and climate determine the rhythm of life here, making it unique.

What To Do

Take Time To Enjoy The Outdoors: Take advantage of the great weather and landscapes to enjoy outdoor activities. I made it a routine to go on morning hikes in local places like Papago Park, where I could watch the sun rise over the desert and reflect golden light on the renowned red rocks.

Attend Local Events: Phoenix has a lively arts and cultural scene, including art walks and music festivals. I went to a First

Friday event in the Roosevelt Row Arts District, where galleries opened their doors for an evening of art and culture. The excitement was contagious, and I met some incredible local artists.

What Not To Do

Don't Isolate Yourself: Spending too much time exploring can prevent you from experiencing the city's social scene. Engage with the locals, strike up conversations, and be open to new opportunities. Some of my fondest recollections stem from conversations with folks I met along the road.

Avoid Overdoing It: When exploring the desert, it's important to pace oneself. I was fatigued after back-to-back hiking days. It is totally OK to take a break and spend a quiet afternoon in a neighborhood café or park.

Reflection: As my time in Phoenix drew to a conclusion, I felt grateful for the opportunities and lessons I had learned. This city is a mix of varied cultures, gorgeous surroundings, and friendly, inviting people.

Phoenix is a location that encourages exploration and interaction. Knowing what to do and what not to do will ensure that your vacation is more than just a list of sights, but rather a genuine experience that leaves a lasting impression on your heart.

So, while you plan your own journey in Arizona's capital, remember to appreciate Phoenix's lively vitality. Engage with its people, experience its delicacies, and enjoy the desert's beauty. The memories you make will certainly be gems from your adventure, brightening it long after you leave.

CHAPTER 5

SCOTTSDALE

What To Do And Not To Do In This Desert Oasis

Scottsdale, nestled against the magnificent McDowell Mountains, is a destination where desert meets modern sophistication. This dynamic city, often known as a "desert oasis," is renowned for its magnificent resorts, world-class golf courses, and thriving art scene. During my recent visit, I fell in love with Scottsdale's unique combination of natural beauty and urban charm. However, traversing this fascinating city demands some information to ensure you get the most of your visit. Allow me to share my adventures and the lessons

I've learnt about what to do and what to avoid in this incredible location.

Key Attractions

Scottsdale is full of attractions that represent its distinct blend of history, culture, and natural beauty. During my exploration, two locations stood out: Old Town and the Scottsdale Museum of Contemporary Art. Each has its own distinct flavor, and I recommend trying both.

Old Town Scottsdale: Old Town is Scottsdale's beating heart, a dynamic region that emits a quaint, rustic ambiance while celebrating the city's Western heritage. As I strolled the cobblestone streets, I was transported into a world that felt both old and new—a place where cowboy tradition meets modern refinement.

What To Do

Stroll Through The Shops: I enjoyed strolling through the stores, which included boutiques, art galleries, and souvenir shops. The selection is vast, ranging from handmade jewelry to local art. I stumbled into The Paper Heart, a little shop where I found gorgeous stationery and unusual gifts made by local artisans. Supporting small companies and discovering unexpected treasures made my shopping experience extremely delightful.

Visit The Scottsdale Waterfront: Visit the Scottsdale Waterfront for breathtaking views of the Arizona Canal and a relaxing walk. I took a coffee from a local café and relaxed while I watched the ducks paddle across the water. It's an ideal location for photographs, especially as the sun begins to set and casts a warm glow over the ocean.

Check Out The Art Walk: Don't miss Scottsdale's Art Walk on Thursday evenings. The galleries open their doors to the public, displaying new exhibits and providing refreshments and music. I socialized with other art aficionados, admired the ingenuity on exhibit, and even had the opportunity to speak with some artists about their work.

What Not To Do

Don't Skip The History: Don't miss out on Scottsdale's rich history, even if you're busy shopping or dining. I made a point of visiting the Scottsdale Historical Museum, where I learnt about the area's Native American origins and settlers' histories. It deepened my comprehension of the place.

Avoid Chain Restaurants: Old Town offers unique dining options, so avoid the temptation to eat at recognized chains. I tried The Mission, a local favorite that serves superb modern Mexican cuisine. Dining at restaurants like these not only benefits local businesses, but also allows you to sample the flavors that distinguish Scottsdale.

Scottsdale Museum Of Contemporary Art: The Scottsdale Museum of Contemporary Art (SMoCA) is conveniently located near Old Town. This modern jewel features unique works from both local and international artists. My visit to the museum was a delightful journey through creativity and contemporary thought.

What To Do

Explore The Exhibits: The diverse paintings displayed in the sleek, minimalist galleries intrigued me. From breathtaking installations to thought-provoking sculptures, each item told a narrative. One exhibit that particularly struck me was a collection of images depicting the changing landscapes of the American Southwest, inspiring thought on our relationship with nature and the environment.

Attend A Workshop Or Event: Attend the museum's workshops, lectures, and film screenings. During my visit, I took part in a guided art-making session, which allowed me to make my own work inspired by the displays. It provided a unique method for me to engage with the art community while also expressing my own talent.

Relax At The Rooftop Garden: Enjoy breathtaking views of the surrounding mountains and metropolis. I found a peaceful location to relax, surrounded by lovely desert plants, and took some time to reflect on my experiences. It was a nice refuge in the midst of the museum's artistic activity.

What Not To Do

Don't Rush Through The Museum: When visiting a museum, it's tempting to rush through, but instead, take your time. Each piece of art tells a narrative, and I discovered that slowing to truly enjoy them enhanced my experience. I spent more than an hour roaming and pondering on the paintings, which was well worth it.

Avoid Visiting On Mondays: Avoid visiting on Mondays as SMoCA is closed, so plan accordingly. I almost made that mistake, but a quick check of their hours spared me from being disappointed by a closed sign on the door.

Getting Around Scottsdale

One of the most enjoyable aspects of touring Scottsdale is its accessibility. Whether you're going to Old Town, the museum, or one of the city's gorgeous parks, getting around is simple.

What To Do

Use A Bicycle: Scottsdale has bike lanes and rental alternatives. I rented a bike from a local store and went for a nice ride down the Arizona Canal, taking in the magnificent scenery and getting some exercise. The fresh wind and sunshine made for an unforgettable experience.

Walk: Many sites, particularly in Old Town, are easily accessible on foot. I frequently found myself walking from one location to another, taking in the local environment. Walking allowed me to enjoy the environment while also discovering secret jewels tucked away in alleyways.

What Not To Do

Don't Miss The Desert Trails: Although the city is beautiful, the neighboring desert provides excellent trekking options. I made an effort to explore paths such as the Gateway Loop Trail in the McDowell Sonoran Preserve. The stunning vistas of the desert terrain, particularly at sunrise and sunset, are not to be missed.

Avoid Driving During Peak Hours: Rush hour traffic can be annoying in any city. To ensure a smoother journey, I found it prudent to schedule my excursions during off-peak hours.

Dining In Scottsdale

Scottsdale's food scene is a delicious blend of flavors that reflects its eclectic culture. From casual restaurants to luxury dining, there's something for everyone.

What To Do

Try Local Specialties: Try local specialties with Southwestern flair. One evening, I ate at Steak 44, where the steak was well cooked and the accompanying sides featured seasonal produce. The experience felt luxurious, but it was the robust tastes that really stood out.

Explore The Brunch Scene: Scottsdale has a vibrant brunch scene, with numerous restaurants offering imaginative and delectable menus. Farm & Craft quickly became one of my favorite places for a fresh and healthy start to the day, thanks to their avocado toast and wonderful smoothies.

What Not To Do

Don't Skip Reservations: Make reservations for popular restaurants, especially during peak tourist seasons, to avoid missing out. I discovered this the hard way when I went up at a few eateries only to find them completely booked.

Avoid Eating Indoors All The Time: While Scottsdale has great indoor dining alternatives, enjoy the gorgeous weather. Many restaurants provide outdoor sitting with breathtaking views, and I frequently chose to dine outside to enjoy the warm desert evenings.

Embracing The Scottsdale Vibe

During my time in Scottsdale, I grew to love not only the sights, but also the city's relaxed, inviting atmosphere. It's a place where rest and adventure coexist, and adopting that mindset made my experience even more delightful.

What To Do

Participate In Local Events: Consider attending local activities like farmers' markets, art fairs, and music festivals. I discovered a small artisan fair one weekend and liked exploring homemade things while socializing with the pleasant people. The community spirit was contagious, and it strengthened my ties to the place.

Take Time For Self-Care: Take time for self-care in Scottsdale, known for its spas and wellness retreats. I rejuvenated myself with a spa day at a local resort. A massage and a session in the sauna left me feeling rested and refreshed, the ideal way to refuel after days of exploring.

What Not To Do

Avoid Rushing Your Experience: While traveling, it's tempting to get caught up in checking off sites on a list. I discovered that slowing down and relishing each minute resulted in deeper experiences. Take time to breathe in the desert air and absorb the natural beauty around you.

Avoid Being Closed-Minded: To avoid being closed-minded, be open to trying new things, whether it's a new food or an activity outside your comfort zone. I surprised myself by attending a pottery lesson at a local studio, which turned out to be one of the trip's highlights.

Reflection: As my Scottsdale adventure came to a close, I felt a deep gratitude for the city and the experiences I experienced. From the creative flair of Old Town to the peacefulness of the Scottsdale Museum of Contemporary Art, every moment served as a reminder of the desert oasis's beauty and diversity.

Scottsdale is a destination that encourages discovery and interaction. Knowing what to do and what not to do helps ensure that your stay is more than just seeing things, but also generating significant memories that will last long after you depart.

So, while you plan your trip to Scottsdale, remember to enjoy the spirit of this incredible city. Engage with its culture, experience its cuisine, and take in the stunning desert landscape. The treasures you find here will surely enhance your trip experience, leaving you with a sense of wonder and a desire to return.

CHAPTER 6

SEDONA

What To Do And Not Do In The Red Rocks

Ah, Sedona—where the soil appears to glow in bright shades of scarlet and orange, and the air vibrates with an otherworldly energy. Nestled amidst northern Arizona's spectacular red rock formations, this charming village is more than simply a feast for the eyes; it's also a spiritual haven. My recent vacation to Sedona awakened my heart and mind to the area's natural beauty, spirituality, and unique adventures. From the breathtaking scenery to the spiritual vortexes, this location has a lot to offer, yet there are some things to embrace and others to shun. Here's my tour of Sedona, highlighting what to do and what to skip while immersed in the magic of this red-rock wonderland.

Key Attractions

Sedona is known for its magnificent red rocks and spiritual atmosphere, which attract visitors from all over the world. During my visit to Sedona, the Chapel of the Holy Cross and Slide Rock State Park were two must-see destinations that truly captured the essence of the area. Each location provides a distinct experience, highlighting the natural beauty and charm of this magnificent place.

Chapel Of The Holy Cross: The Chapel of the Holy Cross, perched on a cliff, is an architectural marvel that seamlessly combines spirituality with nature. As I approached this landmark site, I was fascinated by how it emerges from the rock face, appearing to be a natural extension of the terrain.

What To Do

Take In The Views: Upon entering the chapel, I was met by expansive views that seemed to last forever. The massive windows frame the spectacular red rock formations, producing a breathtaking backdrop that makes you feel like you're a part of the scenery. I spent time simply sitting in the seats, taking in the tranquility of the setting and absorbing the spectacular views. If you're an early riser, watching the sunrise from the chapel is an experience you won't forget.

Explore The Grounds: The chapel's exterior is as magnificent as its inside. I went down the paths that weave around the surrounding cliffs, admiring the meticulously maintained gardens. The sound of the wind rustling through the trees, combined with the distant chirping of birds, provided a serene atmosphere that allowed you to become lost in thinking. Bring your camera; there are plenty of photo chances here.

What Not To Do

Don't Rush Your Visit: This isn't a location to just tick off your list and leave. I discovered that giving me time to really absorb the atmosphere increased my appreciation for the chapel. Set aside some time to fully immerse yourself in the experience, whether you're reflecting in quiet or snapping photos.

Avoid Distracting Attire: While there is no strict dress code in Sedona, tourists tend to dress comfortably and respectfully. I chose breathable textiles and a wide-brimmed hat to protect myself from the sun while remaining casual and observant of my surroundings.

Slide Rock State Park: A short drive from the chapel takes you to Slide Rock State Park, a natural water park ideal for a fun-filled day of exploration. Nestled in Oak Creek Canyon, this park is well-known for its treacherous red rock slides and cooling waters, making it a popular destination for both families and adrenaline seekers.

What To Do

Enjoy The Natural Waterslides: The park's famous natural slides were the highlight of my stay. I joined the other adventurers in sliding down the smooth, polished rocks into the refreshing waters of Oak Creek. It was a wonderful rush, and the laughing and excitement surrounding me were contagious. Wear water shoes for grip and comfort; believe me, they make all the difference.

Take A Scenic Hike: Explore the park's scenic hiking paths, which give breathtaking views of the canyon and surrounding red cliffs. I chose the Canyon Trail, which meanders through gorgeous countryside. The pleasant smell of pine and the sound of rustling leaves enhanced the attraction. Along the trip, I noticed various colorful wildflowers and shot numerous photos to capture the beauty of the area.

What Not To Do

Don't Forget Sunscreen: To protect myself from the harsh Arizona heat, I applied sunscreen throughout the day. Even if it feels nice to splash in the water, the sun might creep up on you. I made this error on my first day and had to learn the hard way.

Avoid Peak Times: Avoid peak times by visiting on weekdays or early mornings. The park can become fairly crowded, especially during the summer months. I arrived early and grabbed a fantastic place near the ocean, allowing me to enjoy a few hours of peace before the crowds arrived.

Embracing The Sedona Experience

Aside from the main sights, Sedona provides an experience that immerses you in its natural beauty and spiritual aura. The town itself is dynamic, with local stores, art galleries, and restaurants reflecting the area's distinct culture.

What To Do

Explore Local Art: Explore Sedona's vibrant arts community by visiting local galleries. I was charmed by the breathtaking vistas depicted by local painters, each painting expressing a narrative about the majestic surroundings. The Tlaquepaque Arts & Crafts Village is a wonderful destination, with beautiful stores and galleries nestled within an elegant Spanish-inspired courtyard. I couldn't resist purchasing a piece of art to commemorate my time in Sedona.

Savor Local Flavors: Sedona's food scene offers a sensory experience. Enjoy local flavors. I had a lovely evening at Mariposa, where the breathtaking vistas were almost as amazing as the food. Their sophisticated take on Latin-inspired cuisine was a feast for the senses, and I made sure to try their famous dessert—a molten chocolate cake that was pure perfection.

What Not To Do

Don't Miss The Sunset: Don't miss Sedona's spectacular sunsets, which are a must-see. Find a nice vantage point, such as Airport Mesa, to watch the sun set below the horizon, illuminating the red rocks in vivid orange and pink. I made the mistake of thinking I could avoid it, but after seeing the gorgeous scenery, I realized why it's a must-do.

Avoid Being Rushed: Travelers may feel compelled to adhere to a rigorous itinerary. I discovered that allowing for spontaneous moments—whether it was stopping in a shop, conversing with people, or simply sitting quietly on a rock—enriched my experience. Sedona has a way of making you want to slow down and appreciate the beauty around you.

Connecting To Sedona's Spiritual Side

Sedona is famed for its spiritual vortexes, which are thought to produce energy that promotes healing and meditation. While I hadn't planned to explore this element of Sedona, I found myself pulled to it, wanting to learn more about its mystical reputation.

What To Do

Visit A Vortex Site: During my time in Sedona, I visited Bell Rock, a well-known vortex site. I had an evident sense of tranquility when I hiked up to the foot of the rock sculpture. Many guests sit or stand in these spots to meditate or just soak up the vibe. I joined a group of like-minded seekers, and we discussed our aims while taking in the scenery. The experience was both grounded and inspiring.

Engage In A Healing Session: I treated myself to a sound healing session at a nearby wellness center. The experience included reclining on a mat as the music of Tibetan singing bowls filled the room. The vibrations resonated deeply within me, bringing a sense of calm that I hadn't expected. If you're open to it, looking into wellness services in Sedona can bring a special dimension to your trip.

What Not To Do

Don't Approach Vortex Sites With Skepticism: Avoid skepticism when visiting vortex sites. Being receptive to the experience made a significant impact. Allow oneself to be interested and free of preconceived notions. Even if you're dubious, enjoying the trip can lead to surprising discoveries.

Avoid Overlooking Local Guides: If you want to understand more about the vortexes or spiritual practices, try taking a guided tour. I participated in a tour given by a local guide who explained the history and significance of the vortex sites, which expanded my awareness of the land and its energy.

Final Reflections: As I concluded my stay in Sedona, I couldn't help but feel wonder and appreciation. The red rocks, spiritual energy, and warmth of the local community all contributed to a memorable experience for me. Sedona is more than just a vacation; it's an exploration of nature's beauty and the spirit of self-discovery.

My visit taught me that the greatest unforgettable experiences are frequently the result of being present in the moment and embracing the beauty all around. Sedona captured my heart and spirit, whether I was sliding down natural rock formations, meditating amidst the red rocks, or watching a sunset that appeared to set the sky ablaze.

As you plan your own vacation in this magnificent place, remember to take time to explore, interact, and ponder. The items you discover along the route will definitely leave a lasting impression, complementing your tour through

Sedona's breathtaking scenery and lively culture. So go explore, and let the red rocks inspire your soul.

CHAPTER 7

FLAGSTAFF

What To Do And Not To Do In This Mountain Town

Flagstaff, located in the heart of northern Arizona, is a hidden gem that mixes the attraction of outdoor activities with a rich tapestry of culture and history. When I first saw this bustling mountain village, surrounded by tall pines and rocky peaks, I felt a strong connection. It is a site where nature and science coexist together, and I was excited to discover its many facets. Flagstaff offers activities for everyone, from stargazing at the Lowell Observatory to trekking the magnificent trails of Walnut Canyon National Monument. However, as with any trip, there are some must-dos and don'ts to ensure your visit is as enjoyable as possible.

Key Attractions

Flagstaff is well-known for its gorgeous landscapes and rich history, with attractions catering to both outdoor enthusiasts and culture seekers. Lowell Observatory and Walnut Canyon National Monument were two of my favorite places to visit during my vacation. Each area offered a fresh perspective on the natural and historical attractions of this wonderful town.

Lowell Observatory: Flagstaff has a rich astronomical past, and a visit to the Lowell Observatory is a must. Percival Lowell, an astronomer, founded this observatory in 1894, and it has served as a beacon of cosmic exploration for nearly 100 years. As I made my way to the observatory, the prospect of staring into the cosmos filled me with excitement.

What To Do

Join A Guided Tour: Learn about the observatory's history and significant findings. I learned about the historic Pluto finding and Flagstaff's crucial role in astronomy research. Our tour guide was really knowledgeable, and I enjoyed how he presented stories that brought the observatory's history to life. If possible, try to take a tour at sunset; watching the sky change from vivid oranges to deep indigos was breathtaking.

Stargazing: Stargazing was the highlight of my visit. The observatory hosts public viewing nights where visitors can peek through its ancient telescopes. I remember being in wonder when I peered up at the moon's crisp and clear craters and even saw Saturn's rings. The crew was cheerful, encouraging us to ask questions as they pointed us constellations and astronomical objects. Dress warmly; the mountain air can cool you as night falls.

What Not To Do

Don't Skip The History: I spent time in the observatory museum. I initially assumed I'd breeze through, but the exhibits were captivating. They provided a deep dive into astronomical history, with artifacts and images depicting humanity's struggle to comprehend the universe. My advice? Spend some time here before venturing out into the night sky.

Avoid High Expectations Of Visibility: Avoid expecting high visibility due to variable weather, especially in hilly places. On my first night, cloud cover covered several astronomical objects. While the personnel did their best to find what was apparent, I discovered that it is vital to remain adaptable. Even if you don't get to view all you wanted, the experience of being among other stargazers and taking in the ambiance is wonderful.

Walnut Canyon National Monument: A short journey from Flagstaff takes you to Walnut Canyon National Monument, a gorgeous place that commemorates the intriguing history of the ancient Puebloans. This place exudes charm and mystery, with its breathtaking cliffs and ancient homes that appear to whisper stories from years past.

What To Do

Explore The Island Trail: Hike through the canyon to see old cliff houses. The trail is short but full of natural beauty and historical background. As I descended, the varied scenery made me feel like I was going back in time. The air was chilly and crisp, and I couldn't help but stop regularly to take photos and enjoy the scenery. The homes are well-preserved and give visitors a look into the lives of the Sinagua people who once lived here.

Visit The Visitor Center: To prepare for the hikes, I visited the Visitor Center first. The exhibits were instructive, providing context for the canyon's ecosystem and the people who lived there. I found the park rangers to be quite friendly and willing to offer their knowledge. They pointed out various aspects of the landscape that I may have overlooked on my own.

What Not To Do

Don't Underestimate The Hike: Don't underestimate the difficulty of the Island Trail hike, despite its small length. I wore strong hiking shoes and packed plenty of water, which made a big difference. If you're not in excellent shape, take your time and enjoy the experience. I noticed several folks rushing, which detracted from their whole experience.

Avoid Littering: As a tourist, I felt a strong obligation to preserve the natural beauty of Walnut Canyon. There are posters encouraging everyone to pack out what they bring in, and I joined the group of careful visitors. Leaving no trace is more than simply being kind; it is critical for maintaining these breathtaking landscapes for future generations.

Embracing Flagstaff's Unique Vibe

Beyond the obvious attractions, Flagstaff has a vibrant cultural scene, local breweries, and lovely boutiques that reflect the town's distinct culture. Each second spent walking the streets revealed unexpected jewels that enhanced my experience.

What To Do

Explore Historic Downtown: Explore Flagstaff's lovely downtown area, which combines ancient and modern structures. I traveled down Route 66, stopping at businesses and art galleries. The local artisans displayed their work, and I saw a stunning piece of pottery that I simply had to bring home. Don't pass up the opportunity to try local cuisine at one of the cafes—my favorite was a cute small restaurant where I ate a fantastic green chili burrito that left me craving more.

Visit Local Breweries: I explored Flagstaff's growing craft beer sector by visiting several local breweries. Mother Road Brewing Company rapidly became my favorite due to its inviting atmosphere and delicious beers. I tasted their Tower Station IPA, which was a welcome treat after a day of climbing. Many breweries provide tours, so if you're interested in the brewing process, ask!

What Not To Do

Don't Miss Local Events: Check out the local event schedule before your vacation to avoid missing out on any activities. I discovered the Flagstaff ArtWalk, a monthly event that highlights local artists and their work. The atmosphere was upbeat, with live music filling the air as visitors moved from art to gallery. During this event, I felt a strong feeling of community, which reminded me that Flagstaff is more than simply a stop on the way—it's a lively, alive town full of talent and enthusiasm.

Avoid Fast Food Chains: Avoid fast food chains and discover the local culinary culture. Flagstaff is full of flavor and variety. I uncovered hidden gems such as food trucks, intimate diners, and upmarket restaurants. Trying local foods, particularly those inspired by southern flavors, is an enjoyable experience.

Connecting With Nature

Flagstaff is an outdoor lover's dream, with unlimited possibilities to hike, bike, and explore the great outdoors. The nearby Coconino National Forest has an abundance of paths and breathtaking beauty that I couldn't pass up.

What To Do

Hiking The San Francisco Peaks: During my visit to Flagstaff, I hiked the Humphreys Peak Trail to Arizona's highest peak, San Francisco Peaks. The trail is difficult, but the views from the summit are nothing short of spectacular. Standing on the peak, surrounded by a sea of mountains, I had an incredible sense of accomplishment. The track is well-marked, and I took the time to enjoy the varied scenery along the way.

Bike The Arizona Trail: If you enjoy biking, I highly recommend checking out the Arizona Trail. I hired a mountain bike and rode a lovely section of this lengthy track that goes through Flagstaff's breathtaking scenery. The excitement of pedaling through towering woods and steep terrain was palpable. I also had the opportunity to observe some great animals along the trip!

What Not To Do

Don't Ignore Weather Conditions: Flagstaff's height causes rapid weather changes, particularly in the mountains. I learned to check the forecast before leaving, and I always packed an extra layer just in case. I encountered a dramatic temperature drop while trekking, which reminded me of the importance of being prepared.

Avoid Straying From Designated Trails: To conserve the ecology, it's important to stick to designated pathways when exploring outdoors. Going off-path might result in erosion and damage to delicate plants. I was proud to be a responsible visitor, which increased my sense of interacting with nature.

Final Thoughts: Flagstaff captivated my heart with its magnificent scenery, rich history, and vibrant community spirit. From the breathtaking views at Lowell Observatory to the ancient houses of Walnut Canyon, every moment spent here deepened my comprehension of this fascinating region. This alpine town is a beautiful combination of adventure and culture, with something for everyone to enjoy.

As I prepared to depart, I reflected on the memories I'd created—the laughter shared with fellow travelers, the breathtaking landscapes, and my increased respect for the grandeur of the universe. Flagstaff is more than just a place to visit; it is an experience that will stay with you long after you leave.

If you find yourself in northern Arizona, spend some time to explore Flagstaff. Accept its outdoor experiences, savor local flavors, and let yourself be taken away by the splendor of this mountain village. Each walk through its streets and trails reveals the warmth and charm that make Flagstaff a memorable stop on any travel.

CHAPTER 8

GRAND CANYON NATIONAL PARK

What To Do And Not To Do At This Natural Wonder

I felt a rush of exhilaration as I reached the Grand Canyon National Park entrance. The Grand Canyon is more than simply a tourist destination; it's a stunning tapestry of nature's handiwork, carved over millennia by the inexorable force of the Colorado River. I had envisioned myself standing on the rim, gazing out into the great expanse of colorful rock layers that tell the tale of Earth's history. This natural wonder, one of the seven natural wonders of the world, drew me in with its spectacular views, awe-inspiring geology, and limitless options for adventure.

Key Attractions

While there is much to see at the Grand Canyon, two highlights of my vacation were the South Rim and the Bright Angel Trail. Each position provided a new view of the canyon's majesty, allowing me to immerse myself in its splendor while also understanding its significance on a natural and cultural level.

The Southern Rim: The South Rim is the most accessible section of the Grand Canyon, and for good reason. As I drove past the park's entrance, I was stunned by the canyon's sheer size. It felt like I'd entered another universe, where the earth opened up to expose deep canyons and bright hues that changed with the sun.

What To Do

Visit Mather Point: My first visit was Mather Point, a popular viewpoint that provides panoramic views of the canyon. As I stood on the brink, I couldn't believe my eyes. The vast expanse of red, orange, and brown hues stretched eternally, providing a magnificent contrast to the blue sky. I watched the sunshine dance across the canyon walls, revealing layers of rock formed over millions of years. Mather Point is extremely popular, so I arrived early in the morning to avoid crowds. The peacefulness of morning was captivating, and I cherished the moment with my camera in hand, catching the changing light.

Explore The Visitor Center: Explore the Grand Canyon Visitor Center, which was a highlight. The informative exhibits helped me obtain a better understanding of the canyon's geology and ecosystem. The rangers were passionate in sharing their knowledge. I learnt about the local plant and animal species, as well as the Native American tribes that have been here for thousands of years. If possible, attend a ranger-led discussion; they are full of great anecdotes and insights that add to the overall experience.

Catch The Sunset At Hopi Point: Visit Hopi Point to catch the sunset, a must-do activity. I arrived early to ensure a nice spot, and I wasn't disappointed. As the sun set, the canyon walls became a brilliant painting of purples, oranges, and reds. The atmosphere was exciting, with other travelers oohing and aahing at the show. It was a magical moment that reminded me of the beauty of nature and our relationship with it.

What Not To Do

Don't Go Beyond The Guardrails: The Grand Canyon is spectacular, but it can also be deadly. As I strolled along the rim, I observed a few people going outside the designated zones to get a better view. While I understand the temptation, it is critical to remain inside the safe parameters. The canyon's precipitous fall are dangerous, and accidents can occur in a moment. Enjoy the views from the viewpoints; there's no need to jeopardize your safety for a photograph.

Avoid Crowds By Timing Your Visit: To avoid crowds, visit the Grand Canyon during off-peak times. I discovered that early mornings and late evenings provided a more tranquil experience. If possible, schedule your vacation for the shoulder seasons, such as spring or fall, when the weather is still great but the crowds are smaller. This allows you to take in the beauty without feeling rushed or overwhelmed.

Bright Angel Trail: After taking in the breathtaking views from the rim, I felt compelled to explore the canyon more intimately. The Bright Angel Trail enticed me with promises of adventure and discovery. This spectacular trail descends from the canyon's rim into its core, allowing visitors to explore its depths.

What To Do

Hiking The Bright Angel Trail: I started my descent early in the morning while the air was still chilly and crisp. The path is well-kept and has several rest spots, which I welcomed as I headed down. The vistas were nothing short of breathtaking; with each switchback, I felt as if I was discovering a new aspect of the canyon. I took my time, pausing regularly to take photos and talk with other hikers. Along the trip, I saw amazing views, abundant foliage, and even some wildlife, such as squirrels and birds darting through the trees. It's crucial to remember that the journey down is easier than the hike up; I appreciated the rest stops where I could collect my breath and enjoy the scenery.

Stop At Indian Garden: About halfway down the walk, I came across Indian Garden, a verdant sanctuary encircled by high rocks. It felt like a hidden jewel in the canyon. I took a break here, eating a snack and taking in the beauty of my surroundings. The garden is an excellent place to unwind and recharge before carrying on. Many hikers turn back from here, but I felt energized and continued on to Plateau Point for even more breathtaking vistas.

Enjoy The View At Plateau Point: During my hike, I reached Plateau Point for a stunning view of the inner canyon and the Colorado River below. Standing at this vantage point, I felt a sense of accomplishment and wonder rush over me. The sight of the river snaking through the canyon was a powerful reminder of the forces that produced this scene. The views from Plateau Point are just spectacular, making the extra effort worthwhile.

What Not To Do

Don't Underestimate The Hike: Remember to pace yourself when hiking the Bright Angel Trail. The return hike can be more difficult than it appears. I made careful to have lots of water and snacks, but I also took breaks when necessary. Hydration is essential in the arid desert climate, so keep a check on your water supplies. A wise hiker once told me, "What goes down must come up," and I took his advise to heart!

Avoid Hiking In The Heat Of The Day: To escape the heat, plan your hike during early morning or late afternoon. The sun beat down hard on my climb back up, and I found myself taking more pauses than I had planned. The canyon's splendor is worth seeing, but remember to listen to your body and be aware of the weather conditions. If you plan to walk during the summer, be prepared for extreme heat and bring suitable gear to keep you safe.

Embracing The Grand Canyon Experience

Beyond the prominent sights, I realized that the Grand Canyon has a rich history and culture. The legacy of Native American tribes such as the Havasupai, Hualapai, and Navajo lends an important degree of significance to this natural wonder.

What To Do

Engage With Native American Culture: I researched the history of Native Americans in the Grand Canyon. Visiting the

Tusayan Ruin and Museum was educational, as it showcased the lives of the ancient Puebloans who lived in the area. The exhibitions offered insight into their culture, values, and relationship to the land. I was attracted by the stories about resilience and harmony with nature.

Attend A Cultural Performance: Consider seeing a cultural performance during your vacation. I was privileged to see a traditional dance performance at the Grand Canyon Visitor Center. The artists told their stories through dance and song, giving me an insight into the diverse culture of Native American tribes. It was a striking reminder of the communities' deep connection to the land and their ongoing presence in the area.

What Not To Do

Don't Overlook The Importance Of Respect: Respect is essential when visiting sacred terrain. It is critical to be aware of cultural sensitivities and avoid actions that could be interpreted as disrespectful. For example, avoid snapping photos at religious places or disrupting ceremonies. Respect for the land and its inhabitants enhances your experience and honors their legacy.

Avoid Littering: Respect the Grand Canyon's fragile beauty and leave no trace during your visit. I brought my trash with me and urged others to do the same. The park's staff works hard to keep this natural beauty clean, and as visitors, we have a responsibility to help conserve it for future generations.

Conclusion: My experience at Grand Canyon National Park was nothing short of transformative. Standing on the rim, going into its depths, and learning about its rich cultural history helped me to form a deep connection with this natural wonder. The vivid hues, grandeur of the environment, and echoes of old cultures left an indelible impression on my heart.

As I prepared to leave, I felt a strong sense of appreciation for the experiences I had shared with other tourists and for the natural beauty I had seen. The Grand Canyon is more than simply a tourist destination; it exemplifies the power of nature and the significance of protecting our planet's natural beauties.

If you visit the Grand Canyon, take the time to explore its many facets. Embrace the adventure, respect the earth, and be inspired by the canyon's grandeur.

CHAPTER 9

TUCSON

What To Do And Not To Do In The Old Pueblo

When I first arrived in Tucson, I was greeted by the warmth of the desert sun, but it was the vibrant culture and rich history that captivated my heart. Tucson, nestled in a valley surrounded by five mountain ranges, is affectionately known as the Old Pueblo, a moniker that evokes the spirit of the original peoples and Spanish settlers who established the city's character. It's a place where the past and the present coexist, where historic adobe buildings stand proudly beside modern establishments and the perfume of southwestern food fills the air.

As I toured Tucson, I realized that it is more than simply a stopover; it is a destination full of adventures, outdoor excursions, and cultural gems. From the breathtaking scenery of Saguaro National Park to the captivating exhibits of the Arizona-Sonora Desert Museum, I felt as if every turn revealed something new and interesting.

Key Attractions

Let's look at what makes Tucson such a wonderful place. The two main attractions I'd like to highlight are Saguaro National Park and the Arizona-Sonora Desert Museum. Each site offers a unique perspective on the region's natural beauty and cultural legacy.

Saguaro National Park: Saguaro National Park exemplifies the Sonoran Desert's natural splendor. I drove through the park's entrance, and the image that met me was pure magic: huge saguaro cactus towering like old sentinels against the stark, blue sky. It was difficult not to feel amazement as I glanced at these enormous plants, which can live for over 150 years and reach heights of up to 40 feet.

What To Do

Take A Beautiful Drive: I chose the Cactus Forest Drive, an 8-mile loop with stunning vistas of the desert countryside. As I drove, I let down the windows to allow the warm air in, enjoying the earthy scent of the desert. The vistas were just breathtaking: towering saguaros silhouetted against the sun, vivid wildflowers waving in the soft breeze, and the occasional rabbit scurrying across the road. I made frequent stops to photograph the breathtaking scenery, taking in each new perspective.

Hike The Trails: After my drive, I wanted to stretch my legs. I chose the Manning Camp Trail, a modest hike that led me deeper into the park's tranquil beauty. The trail took me through a breathtaking saguaro grove, with arms reaching for the heavens. With each stride, I felt a connection with the place, as if the desert's old spirits were whispering secrets to me. Along the trip, I was fortunate to see some desert wildlife, like lizards sunbathing on rocks and birds flying about in the trees. The views from the hike were breathtaking, especially when I reached the lookout point, which provided a panoramic perspective of the huge desert underneath. It served as a reminder of the vastness and beauty of our area.

Photography Tips: Golden Hour is a must-see for photographers. The greatest time to photograph the renowned saguaro cactus is around daybreak or sunset, when golden light bathes the area. I made a point of setting my alarm early to catch the sunrise, and it was well worth the effort. The gentle light transformed the desert into a painter's palette, casting shadows and highlights that made the saguaros stand out against the vivid sky.

What Not To Do

Don't Underestimate The Desert Heat: Don't underestimate the desert's heat, especially during peak summer months. I packed plenty of water, wore a wide-brimmed hat, and applied sunscreen liberally. Many people underestimate the necessity of hydration, but believe me, you do not want to feel the tiredness that comes from not drinking enough water. Even a short hike can be strenuous in the heat, so stay prepared and listen to your body.

Avoid Climbing On Cacti: Avoid climbing on saguaros, as it is both dangerous and unlawful. The spines can cause painful injuries, and destroying the cacti can result in significant fines. Respect the park's natural beauty and admire the saguaros from a distance.

Arizona-Sonora Desert Museum: Just a short drive from Saguaro National Park, I arrived at the Arizona-Sonora Desert Museum, which much exceeded my expectations. More than just a museum, it is a live, breathing example of the Sonoran Desert ecosystem's beauty and complexity.

What To Do

Explore The Exhibitions: The museum offers a unique mix of indoor and outdoor exhibits. I started my visit by exploring the numerous exhibits that highlight the Sonoran Desert's rich history, flora, and fauna. The live animal exhibitions were very interesting; I marveled at the desert foxes' sleek movements and the brilliant colors of the native birds. Each exhibit was painstakingly created, providing insights into the fragile balance of life in this arid environment.

Stroll Through The Gardens: One of the delights of my vacation was strolling through the museum's gorgeous desert gardens. I was fascinated by the brilliant colors of blossoming cacti and wildflowers. The garden walks are adorned with information plaques that detail the various plants and how they adapt to live in the harsh desert climate. It was a tranquil paradise, and I spent my time admiring the beauty around me. I also saw a few butterflies fluttering amid the flowers, adding to the wonderful atmosphere.

Catch A Raptor Free Flight Show: During my visit, I highly recommend seeing the Raptor Free Flight Show. I sat in the shaded seating area, excited to watch the birds of prey soar overhead. The program was both amusing and educational, with the crew sharing great facts about the many species. I was overjoyed when a gorgeous bird soared close above my head, its wings throwing a shadow over me. It was a thrilling event that demonstrated the beauty and strength of these magnificent birds.

What Not To Do

Don't Rush Your Visit: Do not rush your visit to the Arizona-Sonora Desert Museum. I discovered that I could easily spend all day examining the exhibits, walking the trails, and seeing the shows. I recommend giving yourself plenty of time to take in all that the museum has to offer. The more I stayed, the more I realized how intricately connected the many aspects of the desert environment are.

Avoid Feeding The Animals: It's tempting to interact with the animals, but feeding them is strictly prohibited. It not only harms their health but also interferes with their normal behaviors. The museum staff works hard to provide a safe and natural environment for the animals, so follow their regulations. Enjoy seeing these beautiful creatures from a distance, allowing their natural beauty to speak for themselves.

Embracing Tucson Culture And Cuisine

Beyond its spectacular natural attractions, Tucson has a rich tapestry of culture and food that is worth exploring. I became engaged in the local customs, from art and music to the delectable flavors of southwestern cuisine.

What To Do

Visit The Historic Barrio Viejo: Visit the Historic Barrio Viejo for a nostalgic experience. This historic area features colorful adobe homes and brilliant murals that reflect Tucson's diverse cultural past. I took my time strolling the streets, admiring the distinctive architecture and artistic expressions on the walls. It's a great place to photograph, and I tried to capture the soul of the neighborhood with my camera.

Enjoy The Local Cuisine: I couldn't leave Tucson without sampling its delicious cuisine. The city is well-known for its Sonoran-style food, which combines Mexican flavors with local products. One evening, I ate at a neighborhood restaurant that featured carne asada tacos with fresh guacamole and handmade tortillas. Each bite was a flavor explosion, and I enjoyed the meal while speaking with locals about their favorite meals. Tucson is a UNESCO City of Gastronomy, so don't pass up the opportunity to experience its rich food scene.

Experience Local Festivals: Visit Tucson during one of its festivals to fully immerse yourself in the local culture. From the Tucson Rodeo to the All Souls Procession, these events provide insight into the local culture and communal spirit. I went to the All Souls Procession, which is a wonderful celebration of life and remembrance. The streets were crowded with colorful costumes, music, and art, generating a sense of excitement and unity.

What Not To Do

Don't Ignore Local Customs: When visiting Tucson, it's crucial to respect local customs and traditions. In many local markets and restaurants, it's common to greet personnel with a warm "Hola" or "Buenos días." Embracing the local culture enhances the experience and shows respect for the town you're visiting.

Avoid Chain Restaurants: Tucson has several popular chain restaurants, but the best ones are generally hidden in small areas. I made it a point to seek out family-owned restaurants and food trucks, where I encountered unique sensations that were truly remarkable. Supporting local businesses not only improves your trip experience, but it also contributes to the city's lively culture.

Conclusion: Tucson is a compelling combination of nature, culture, and gastronomic delights. Whether you're hiking through the breathtaking vistas of Saguaro National Park or immersing yourself in the vivid ambiance of the Arizona-Sonora Desert Museum, this city exudes an irresistible appeal.

As I concluded my time to Tucson, I felt grateful for the experiences I had had. The gigantic saguaros, the cultural complexity, and the delectable flavors all carved themselves into my memory, weaving a tapestry of experiences that would stay with me long after I departed. Tucson is more than just a tourist destination; it beckons you to connect, discover, and appreciate the desert's beauty and people. So pack your luggage, grab your camera, and embark on your own journey in the Old Pueblo. Tucson will embrace you with open arms, just as it did for me.

CHAPTER 10

LAKE HAVASU CITY

What To Do And Not To Do By The Water

When I first heard of Lake Havasu City, I imagined a sun-drenched utopia with glistening waters and a touch of eccentric charm. This city, located in the northwest corner of Arizona, is most known for its namesake lake and the magnificent London Bridge—yes, the same bridge that was brought stone by stone from England! I headed out to explore this colorful place, drawn to its distinct blend of natural beauty and whimsical history.

As I approached Lake Havasu City, I was met with panoramic vistas of the lake's azure waters, framed by jagged desert mountains. The sun was high in the sky, putting a pleasant warmth on everything. It was a welcoming setting that offered exploration, relaxation, and a dash of fun. I couldn't wait to experience everything this destination has to offer.

Key Attractions

The London Bridge and Lake Havasu State Park were two of the most memorable attractions in Lake Havasu City. Both places provided a great peek into the city's culture and a variety of activities to enjoy.

London Bridge: The history of the London Bridge is one of luck and genius. I couldn't help but smile as I stood on the bridge, knowing that it was initially erected in London in the 1830s and then disassembled in the 1960s before being rebuilt in Lake Havasu City in 1971. It was a pretty magical experience, and I felt transported across the seas.

What To Do

Take A Stroll Across The Bridge: My initial reaction was to walk across the antique bridge. As I strolled along, I marveled at the architecture and fine details on the stones. With the Colorado River running beneath me, I could see boats passing by, their colorful sails fluttering in the breeze. The vista was spectacular, and I took several shots of the river and the surrounding mountains.

Visit The Bridgewater Channel: Visit the Bridgewater Channel, a scenic waterfront area with shops, restaurants, and parks located on the bridge's west side. I spent some time walking around the bright shops, collecting unique souvenirs and local crafts. There is something magical about a place where people gather to enjoy the water and the bustling environment. I also discovered beautiful restaurants where I could enjoy a leisurely lunch while admiring the views of the bridge and the bustling channel.

Catch A Sunset: Lake Havasu City is known for its breathtaking sunsets. I made a point of returning to the bridge in the evening. The sky turned into a canvas of oranges, pinks, and purples, which reflected brilliantly on the sea. It was a lovely moment, and I was grateful to see such natural beauty.

What Not To Do

Don't Rush Your Visit: When visiting the London Bridge, it's important to take your time and enjoy the experience, rather than rushing through it. Don't rush across the bridge, as I seen many tourists doing. Instead, take a moment to admire the history and beautiful surroundings. Take a moment to soak up the ambiance and let the charm of the location wash over you.

Avoid Feeding Wildlife: I was tempted to feed the ducks near the water, but realized that it can alter their natural behavior and diet. Instead, I kept a safe distance and enjoyed their antics without interfering. Respecting the native species is critical to preserving the lake's sensitive ecosystem.

Lake Havasu State Park: After enjoying my time at the London Bridge, I chose to visit Lake Havasu State Park. This park, which covers 1,200 acres, is ideal for outdoor enthusiasts and environment lovers. As I reached the park, I was met with the lovely sound of waves lapping against the coast and the distant laughing of families spending the day at the lake.

What To Do

Beach Activities: The park has several clean beaches where tourists can relax in the sun or cool off in the lake. I lay out my beach towel on the sand and settled back for some relaxation. After a while, I decided to cool down in the water, where I laid on my back and gazed up at the clear sky. The soft waves swayed me as I closed my eyes and took in the peaceful atmosphere.

Kayaking And Paddleboarding: The lake offers a variety of water sports, including kayaking and paddleboarding, which I was excited to attempt. I rented a kayak from a local outfitter and went out on the water. Paddling around the shoreline allowed me to discover secret coves and inlets, providing a unique viewpoint on the stunning scenery. I felt a thrill of excitement as I navigated the mild currents, noticing colorful fish darting beneath the surface.

Hiking Trails: Following my water exploits, I wanted to explore the land as well. Lake Havasu State Park has various hiking paths that go through the arid environment. I chose the Mojave Desert Trail, a reasonably difficult hike with breathtaking views of the lake from above. As I hiked down the trail, I came across brilliant desert wildflowers and fascinating rock formations. The silence of the desert surrounded me, allowing an opportunity for introspection amidst the splendor of nature.

What Not To Do

Don't Forget The Sunscreen: When visiting Arizona, it's crucial to remember to bring sunscreen to protect your skin from the harsh sun. I developed the habit of using sunscreen on a regular basis, especially after swimming or sweating. You don't want to ruin your vacation by getting a nasty sunburn. Take precautions against the sun, and consider wearing a wide-brimmed hat and UV-protective clothing.

Avoid Littering: While exploring the park, I realized the necessity of maintaining a clean and beautiful environment. Respect for the natural environment is essential, which includes not littering and properly disposing of waste. Lake Havasu City's beauty is a valuable asset that should be protected for future generations. I even brought a tiny bag to pick any rubbish I came across, feeling a sense of obligation to help keep this paradise clean.

Embracing Lake Havasu Lifestyle

Beyond the attractions, what actually made my visit to Lake Havasu City memorable was the community's lifestyle. The relaxed, welcoming atmosphere encouraged me to appreciate local culture and make the most of my surroundings.

What To Do

Join A Local Event: During my vacation, I was fortunate to attend a local event along the lakefront. It was a vibrant event with live music, food vendors, and artisan booths. I interacted with people, ate wonderful street food, and loved the lively atmosphere. It was an excellent chance to feel community spirit and learn more about what makes Lake Havasu City distinct.

Rent A Boat: Renting a boat for a day was a must-do activity to really enjoy the lake experience. I collected a group of pals and ventured out to explore the vast seas of Lake Havasu. The freedom of being on the ocean was exciting! We explored secret coves, swam, and even had a lunch on a little beach. There's something amazing about being on the sea, surrounded by beautiful landscape, and I treasured every moment.

Explore The Local Cuisine: Lake Havasu City has several dining options, ranging from casual to upmarket. I made an effort to savor local cuisines, trying dishes like fish tacos and fresh salads cooked with locally produced vegetables. Dining near the sea was a pleasure, as I ate my lunch while watching boats sail by in the fading light.

What Not To Do

Don't Miss Out On Socializing: Lake Havasu City's warm atmosphere makes it easy to connect with locals. I discovered that the more I interacted with others, the more I learnt about the area's hidden riches. Don't be afraid to make connections; you never know what stories or recommendations you'll discover.

Avoid Staying Indoors: Spending too much time indoors would be a waste given the amazing outside activities available. Lake Havasu City's beauty lies in its landscapes and rivers, so take advantage of the opportunity to explore, relax, and soak up the sun. Every moment spent outside provides an opportunity to make memorable memories.

Conclusion: As my trip to Lake Havasu City came to an end, I felt a profound sense of gratitude for the experiences I had experienced with this stunning location. Every moment of my tour, from the quirky appeal of the London Bridge to the natural beauty of Lake Havasu State Park, enriched my experience.

The city's dynamic atmosphere, combined with its breathtaking landscapes, offered an ideal balance of rest and action. I left Lake Havasu City with a heart full of memories and the resolve to return. If you're looking for a place to explore, relax, and connect, Lake Havasu City is calling your name. It's a location where the water shines, sunsets illuminate the sky, and the spirit of the desert pervades every experience. Pack your luggage and head for this enchanting oasis; I tell you that the adventure of a lifetime awaits.

CHAPTER 11

YUMA

What To Do And Not To Do In The Sunniest City

Yuma, Arizona, is a bustling city located in the southwest part of the state, within a stone's throw from the California border. Yuma, known as the sunniest city in the United States, attracts visitors with its rich history, vibrant culture, and breathtaking surroundings. During my visit, I realized that Yuma is more than simply a rest stop; it's a treasure trove of opportunities waiting to be explored.

When I arrived in Yuma, the first thing I noticed was the vast blue sky above. The desert sun sent a warm glow across the countryside, and I felt its warming embrace. With my plan in hand, I went out to discover the city's top attractions, each with its own distinct narrative to tell.

Key Attractions

Yuma has a plethora of historical landmarks and picturesque areas that cater to a variety of interests. During my vacation, I visited the Yuma Territorial Prison and the Colorado River State Historic Park. Both venues provided great insights into the city's history and allowed me to enjoy the splendor of the Colorado River.

Yuma Territorial Prison: When I entered the Yuma Territorial Prison, I felt like I had been transported back in time. Established in 1876, this historic monument housed some of the most notorious criminals of the Old West. As I strolled through the prison's ancient walls, I imagined the stories of the inmates who had once roamed the grounds.

What To Do

Take A Guided Tour: I chose a guided tour, which was educational and fascinating. The guide, a local historian who is passionate about Yuma's past, regaled us with stories of notorious convicts and spectacular escapes. I learnt about the prison's distinctive architecture, which had thick stone walls and arched windows that provided a view into the brutal realities of life behind bars.

Explore The Museum: After the tour, I explored the on-site museum. The exhibitions featured artifacts from the prison's operations, such as old uniforms, tools, and convicts' personal belongings. One item piqued my interest: a collection of letters written by convicts, full of longing and regret. It was a painful reminder of the human stories that existed behind the prison walls.

Take Photos Of The Ruins: The prison's decaying walls and rusted cells made for stunning photos. I took a few photographs, capturing the sharp contrast between the prison's gloomy past and the bright blue sky above. If you enjoy photography, don't pass up the opportunity to capture this captivating blend of history and current.

What Not To Do

Don't Rush Through Your Visit: Don't rush through your visit to the Yuma Territorial Prison, which has a rich history and deserves your entire attention. I noticed several guests rushing through, barely glancing at the exhibits. Take your time reading the placards and processing the stories. There is so much to learn, and if you go further, you may discover a personal link to the past.

Avoid The Temptation To Climb On The Ruins: Avoid climbing on the jail ruins to preserve its historical integrity. I spotted a few guests climbing the collapsing walls for selfies, but I chose a safer and more respectable angle. It is a common responsibility to preserve history for future generations.

Colorado River State Historical Park: After studying the prison's history, I decided to visit the Colorado River State Historic Park. This stunning park is located directly on the banks of the magnificent Colorado River and offers a delightful blend of nature and history.

What To Do

Enjoy A Scenic Walk: Take a scenic walk along the park's riverside trails, which offer breathtaking views of the surrounding area. I took a leisurely stroll, soaking in the fresh air and admiring the views. The sound of the river running was peaceful, and I found myself pausing frequently to appreciate the beauty of the surroundings.

Visit The Historic Structures: Explore the park's historic structures, such as the Yuma Quartermaster Depot. This structure was critical to military supply in the late nineteenth century. I strolled into the old warehouses, recalling the frenzied bustle that formerly occurred here. The interpretive signs provided useful information about the site's history and relevance in the region.

Picnic By The River: I brought a picnic lunch and found the ideal location along the riverbank. As I settled back for my breakfast, I felt the pleasant air against my skin and listened to the sounds of nature. It was a tranquil moment, and I savored the tastes of my lunch while watching the ducks skim across the river.

What Not To Do

Don't Skip The Visitor Center: Before exploring the park, I highly recommend visiting the Visitor Center. It contains information about the park's history and the surrounding area. I learnt about the Colorado River's role in Yuma's growth, as well as the fauna that lives in the area. Skipping this step would result in a loss of valuable knowledge.

Avoid Littering: Avoid littering to maintain the park's cleanliness and beauty. I saw a few pieces of litter left behind by thoughtless visitors, which marred the otherwise beautiful atmosphere. Make sure to carry out whatever you bring in while respecting the environment. It's a simple deed that contributes significantly to the preservation of Yuma's beauty.

Embracing Yuma Culture

Beyond its historical charms, Yuma provides a distinct cultural experience that enriches each visit. The city offers a thriving artistic scene, delectable culinary choices, and a warm community atmosphere that will make you feel right at home.

What To Do

Explore The Arts District: One evening, I explored Yuma's arts district, which had galleries, studios, and public art works. The streets were alive with color and imagination, and I was impressed by the talent of the local painters. I began conversing with a few artists, who enthusiastically explained their inspirations and the stories behind their creations. It was a lovely way to engage with the local culture and learn about the creative process.

Savor Local Cuisine: Yuma's local cuisine is a must-try during your visit. I sought out local restaurants and food trucks, anxious to try the region's cuisine. From real Mexican street tacos to succulent BBQ, the food scene was a feast for the senses. I made a point of trying the Yuma lettuce, which is known for its sharpness and flavor. Each bite was a delightful reminder of the region's agricultural bounty.

Attend A Local Event: During my visit, I discovered the Yuma Lettuce Days event, which celebrates the region's agricultural riches. The event featured live music, cooking demonstrations, and, of course, a variety of delectable lettuce-inspired foods. I participated in the fun, dancing to upbeat music and eating delicious food. It was an excellent opportunity to interact with locals and immerse myself in Yuma's lively culture.

What Not To Do

Don't Miss Out On Local Recommendations: Yuma residents are pleasant and willing to share their favorite sites and hidden gems. I made a point of asking for recommendations at restaurants and galleries, which led to some fantastic discoveries. Instead of following a tight agenda, be open to serendipity and allow the locals to take you to the best experiences.

Avoid Tourist Traps: While Yuma has many attractions, some feel too commercialized and lack authenticity. Be careful of where you spend your time and choose experiences that speak to you. Seek out sites that capture the authentic essence of Yuma, and you'll leave with genuine and long-lasting memories.

Conclusion: As my time in Yuma came to an end, I felt a deep appreciation for the city's richness and beauty. From the haunting echoes of the Yuma Territorial Prison to the tranquil serenity of the Colorado River, each minute spent here was a part in a greater story about history, culture, and community.

Yuma is a destination that encourages exploration, whether it's roaming around its ancient landmarks, sampling its culinary pleasures, or engaging with the friendly residents. I left with a heart full of memories and a desire to return. Yuma is a must-see location for people looking for adventure as well as a taste of authentic culture. As I drove away, I looked back at the city, the setting sun spreading a golden glow over the landscape, and I knew Yuma's soul would live on in my heart long after I departed.

CHAPTER 12

PRESCOTT

What To Do And Not To Do In Arizona's Mile High City

Prescott, nestled among the rough terrain and towering pines of Arizona's highlands, is a charming place that captured my heart during my travels. Prescott, known as Arizona's "Mile High City" due to its height of more than 5,000 feet, provides a beautiful blend of history, natural beauty, and an attractive small-town feel. From the colorful energy of Whiskey Row to the peaceful trails of the Prescott National Forest, every area of this city has a story waiting to be told.

Key Attractions

During my time in Prescott, I set out to visit its most noteworthy landmarks, each of which provided a unique view into the city's rich history and gorgeous surroundings. I couldn't resist going to Whiskey Row, a historic strip dotted with bustling saloons and stores, and the vast Prescott National Forest, where I could immerse myself in nature's embrace.

Whiskey Row: Whiskey Row is the heart and spirit of Prescott, a lively thoroughfare steeped in Wild West legends. As I walked down the wooden walkways, I sensed the spirit of the old frontier whispering stories about cowboys, gamblers, and gold miners.

What To Do

Visit The Historic Saloons: My first destination was the Palace Restaurant and Saloon, Arizona's oldest saloon, founded in 1877. When I walked through the doors, the mood overwhelmed me—the rich wood paneling, vintage furnishings, and subtle murmur of conversations created a welcoming setting. I ordered a local craft beer and enjoyed the nostalgia of the setting. The pub was a pulsating tapestry of history, with guests laughing and telling stories exactly as they had done over a century before.

Explore The Shops: I visited the quirky shops on Whiskey Row, each selling unique items. From cowboy hats to handmade jewelry, I found myself looking for keepsakes to remind me of my time in Prescott. I stumbled into a modest store selling locally crafted things, where I discovered a lovely hand-painted ornament that now hangs on my Christmas tree as a memento of this enchanting city.

Enjoy Live Music: In the evening, Whiskey Row comes alive with local musicians. I discovered a nice corner at The Bird Cage Saloon, where a band performed classic country songs. The mood was fantastic, with people laughing, dancing, and clinking their drinks. I joined the crowd, tapping my feet to the rhythm and enjoying Prescott's energetic atmosphere.

What Not To Do

Don't Skip The History: Don't miss out on Whiskey Row's rich heritage, despite its lively nightlife. Take a moment to read the historical plaques explaining the significance of each building. I learnt about the unsavory figures who formerly roamed these streets, as well as Prescott's vital role during Arizona's early statehood. Ignoring this feature would be like missing out on the rich tapestry that makes Prescott so unique.

Avoid Overindulging: The abundance of tempting drinks can lead to overindulgence. I noticed a few people who had probably had too many drinks and missed out on the companionship and stories that made the saloons unique. Pace yourself, appreciate the flavors, and ensure that you can fully immerse yourself in the event without losing the night's magic.

Prescott National Forest: After enjoying the bustling environment of Whiskey Row, I felt compelled to visit the gorgeous Prescott National Forest. This vast expanse of pine trees, craggy mountains, and quiet lakes provided a peaceful respite from the city's rush and bustle.

What To Do

Hiking Trails: The Prescott National Forest has hiking paths suitable for all skill levels. I chose the Thumb Butte Trail, a gentle hike that promised beautiful vistas. As I ascended, the air became crisper and the aroma of pine engulfed me. Each step got me closer to the stunning views of the surrounding valleys and mountains. When I reached the summit, I was blessed with an awe-inspiring panoramic vista of nature, pristine and spectacular. Standing there, I felt a strong connection to the land, as if time stood still.

Picnicking By The Lakes: After my hike, I relaxed at Watson Lake, surrounded by granite boulders and towering trees. I stretched out my picnic blanket and ate a lovely supper while admiring the beauty surrounding me. The rhythmic lapping of the river and delicate rustling of leaves formed a soothing soundscape, ideal for unwinding. If you're seeking for a peaceful vacation, this is the place to be.

Wildlife Watching: While exploring the trails, I kept an eye out for the different fauna that inhabits the woodland. I was fortunate to see a family of deer grazing quietly amid the woods, as well as a gorgeous hawk swooping overhead. I even came across a pleasant flock of wild turkeys strutting along the route. Bring your binoculars and take your time; the woodland is full of surprises waiting to be discovered.

What Not To Do

Don't Ignore Trail Etiquette: While hiking, I met several hikers who shared my enthusiasm for the forest's beauty. I made it a point to follow trail etiquette, ceding to those heading upward and keeping noise to a minimum to respect nature's tranquility. I saw a few hikers blasting music and failing to keep their voices down, which took away from the serene mood. Remember, this is a communal location, so step softly and with consideration for the environment and your fellow travelers.

Avoid Leaving Trash Behind: To preserve nature's beauty, it's important to avoid littering along pathways. Prescott National Forest thrives in its pure surroundings, so I took sure to pack out everything I brought in. Keep the forest beautiful for others to enjoy, and leave no evidence of your presence.

Exploring Prescott's Culture

Aside from its attractions, Prescott has a rich cultural heritage that reveals the heart and soul of this wonderful city. The local population is friendly and hospitable, and I was excited to experience the art, food, and customs that make Prescott special.

What To Do

Explore Local Art Galleries: I visited the Prescott Center for the Arts, where local artists showcased their work in various mediums. I was intrigued to a colorful artwork depicting Prescott's scenery. The gallery featured rotating exhibits, so every visit provided new ideas. I started up a chat with a local artist whose work was on display, and she shared her enthusiasm for capturing the splendor of Arizona's sunsets. Participating in the local art scene expanded my experience and increased my respect for the creativity that exists in Prescott.

Sample Local Cuisine: Prescott has a vibrant culinary scene that reflects its many influences. I went to The Raven Café, a popular local restaurant known for its farm-to-table menu. I ordered a great sandwich with locally produced ingredients and sweet potato chips. The café's comfortable atmosphere and courteous personnel made it an ideal place to relax. Don't be afraid to ask locals for recommendations—they're generally willing to share their favorite restaurants and hidden gems.

Attend A Community Event: During my stay, I got the opportunity to visit the local farmer's market. It was a lively gathering full of local vegetables, artisanal goods, and welcoming faces. I ate freshly baked bread and tried homemade jams while talking with farmers about their crops. Events like these give tourists a sense of the community's character and allow them to connect with locals in a meaningful way.

What Not To Do

Don't Miss Out On Festivals: Don't miss out on Prescott's festivals, which celebrate art, music, and food. I discovered that the Prescott Rodeo is a must-see event for everyone traveling in July. Check the local calendar and schedule your vacation around these events; they offer a rich cultural experience that you will not want to miss.

Avoid The Tourist Path: Instead than focusing on popular attractions, consider exploring off-the-beaten-path areas. Some of my most memorable moments in Prescott were when I explored the city's hidden corners, stumbled onto tiny coffee shops, and discovered local art works. Keep your mind open to the unexpected, and you can discover your own favorite areas that resonate with you.

Conclusion: As I prepared to leave Prescott, I felt grateful for the memories I'd made in this beautiful city. My time here had been a beautiful blend of adventure, culture, and connection, from the vibrant energy of Whiskey Row to the peaceful embrace of Prescott National Forest.

Prescott is more than just a destination; it's a location that encourages discovery and participation. The legends of its past and the friendliness of its community have made an unforgettable impression on my heart. Whether you're hiking in the national park, drinking on Whiskey Row, or taking in the local arts scene, Prescott provides an unforgettable experience.

As I drove away, I looked in the rearview mirror and saw the lovely panorama surrounded by the pines. I knew I'd be carrying a piece of Prescott with me wherever I went, as a continual reminder of the beauty that can be found in nature and community. If you find yourself in Arizona, don't pass on this hidden gem; Prescott is waiting to share its story with you.

CHAPTER 13

TOMBSTONE

What To Do And Not To Do In The Town Too Tough To Die

Stepping into Tombstone seemed like stepping back in time—a daring foray into the Wild West, where legends were born and stories of bravery, lawlessness, and grit echoed through the streets. Tombstone, often known as "The Town Too Tough to Die," is rich in history, and each visit promises an adventure mixed with the thrill of the Old West. My voyage to this historic frontier town was filled with enthusiasm and a desire to follow in the footsteps of legendary figures such as Wyatt Earp and Doc Holliday.

Key Attractions

Tombstone has a plethora of attractions that clearly depict its rich history. With each stop, I was entertained while also learning about the events that shaped the American West. The O.K. Corral and Boot Hill Graveyard are unquestionably the centerpieces of this ancient town.

O.K. Corral: No vacation to Tombstone is complete without visiting the renowned O.K. Corral was the site of the infamous shootout on October 26, 1881. The atmosphere was electrifying, like if ghosts from the past were looking over the people who had gathered to see this historic monument.

What To Do

Witness The Reenactment: I arrived just in time to witness a daily reenactment of the gunfight. The performers, dressed in period costumes, transported me back to that terrible day. As the action progressed, I could almost sense the tension in the air. The sound of gunfire, the players' yells, and the reaction of the audience produced an immersive experience that brought history to life. I found myself on the edge of my seat, my heart beating as the drama unfolded in front of me. If you have the chance, sit in the front row—it's the greatest position for all the action!

Explore The Museum: Following the reenactment, I entered the O.K. Visit Corral Museum to discover more about the town's rich past. The exhibits included artifacts, images, and narratives about the circumstances leading up to the gunfight as well as the lives of people involved. I was particularly drawn to the story of the Earp brothers and their tireless pursuit of justice. The museum personnel was extremely knowledgeable, willing to share insights and answer inquiries. I spent about an hour absorbing the history; it was a self-educational experience.

Shop For Souvenirs: Shop for souvenirs in the area surrounding the O.K. Corral is littered with stores that sell cowboy-themed items. I couldn't resist purchasing a few souvenirs, including cowboy hats, fake guns, and even some locally created jewelry. I discovered a delightful tiny shop that sells hand-painted souvenirs and purchased a modest item as a memento of my trip through the Wild West.

What Not To Do

Don't Miss The History: While the reenactments and shopping are exciting, it's important not to overlook the site's historical significance. Take a moment to study the informational plaques located throughout the area. They provide essential context for what you are viewing. A lack of comprehension may result in missing out on the core of this town and the legends it contains.

Avoid Flash Photography: Avoid using flash photography during reenactments since it can distract performers and destroy the ambiance. Remember that while collecting memories is important, being respectful of the performers and the event is also essential. Instead, use natural light and enjoy the present moment.

Boot Hill Graveyard: After immersing myself in the drama of O.K. Corral, I felt obliged to visit the Boot Hill Graveyard. This grave site for some of Tombstone's most notorious people is rich with history and serious thought.

What To Do

Take A Self-Guided Tour: Walking through Boot Hill's worn wooden gates, I was struck by the serene atmosphere. The graves, some inscribed with simple wooden crosses, conveyed the story of lives cut short due to violence, suffering, and the harsh realities of frontier existence. I picked up a self-guided tour leaflet at the entryway, which included information about prominent figures buried there, such as gunfighters and outlaws. Each headstone had a story, and as I read, I could almost hear the whispers of the past all around me. Standing near the grave of Ike Clanton, one of the infamous gunfight participants, I mused on how these people helped build Tombstone's history.

Pay Respect: Boot Hill is more than a tourist attraction; it's a place of memory. I took a moment to silently remember those who died in a town plagued with danger and war. This calm pondering was one of the most moving aspects of my vacation. I spotted a few individuals conversing loudly, which seemed out of place, so I made an effort to keep my voice down, respecting the seriousness of the graves surrounding me.

Capture The Moment: The cemetery's unique grave stones make for beautiful photos. I tried to capture the essence of this eerily beautiful spot without disrupting its peace. The late afternoon sun gave a golden glow across the landscape, lending a mystical look to my photographs. I then utilized these photographs to make a photo album of my trip, with each picture invoking a memory related to the stories I learned.

What Not To Do

Don't Disturb Grave Sites: Taking pictures with grave markers might be rude. Many guests came to pay their respects, and I wanted to make sure I respected the site's heritage. So, instead of posing with the markers, I elected to photograph them and their surroundings. Respect for the deceased is paramount, and a reverent attitude is required.

Avoid Littering: Despite the graveyard's beauty, I noticed rubbish in certain spots. It's critical to leave the area how you found it. I took a moment to pick up a few stray pieces of rubbish, intending to encourage others to do the same. Maintaining Boot Hill's beauty and purity should be everyone's duty.

The Spirit Of Tombstone

Beyond its historical features, Tombstone exudes the Wild West vibe. The streets are lined with wooden buildings, and horse-drawn carriages pass by, giving the impression that I had genuinely stepped back in time.

What To Do

Take A Self-Guided Tour: To learn more about Tombstone's history, I took a guided walking tour. The guide, a local historian, told us stories from the town's heyday during the silver rush. I learned about the infamous gunfights, the rise and collapse of enterprises, and everyday life in the town. Each anecdote provided a clear picture of the difficulties encountered by early settlers. If you have the opportunity, join one of these tours—they're a wonderful way to immerse yourself in local history.

Visit The Bird Cage Theatre: Visit the Bird Cage Theatre, a former theater and brothel. I stepped inside and was overwhelmed by the deep antiquity that clung to the walls. The theater still hosts live plays, and I enjoyed a vibrant reenactment that exemplified the theatrical flair of the era. The spooky atmosphere, along with stories of ghost encounters, created a thrilling experience.

Attend A Local Event: Consider attending local events during your vacation. I was lucky to see a reenactment of the Tombstone Rose Festival, which commemorated the town's heritage and communal spirit. Colorful floats, live music, and delectable local cuisine filled the streets. Engaging with the community made my experience even more memorable.

What Not To Do

Don't Rush During Your Visit: Some people rush through attractions to complete their lists. I discovered that the genuine enchantment of Tombstone is in taking the time to investigate each location and absorb the story. Slow down, absorb the experience, and interact with the inhabitants; you'll come away with a deeper grasp of the town's past.

Avoid Being Disrespectful: Tombstone's history is filled with stories of violence and tragedy. While having a good time is important, being too rowdy or disrespectful might detract from the overall experience. I made an effort to be aware of my surroundings, particularly in quieter locations, to ensure that I respected the essence of the place.

Conclusion: As my stay in Tombstone came to an end, I felt a sense of accomplishment that comes from connecting with history and accepting the stories of the past. This community, with its rustic appeal and enduring spirit, reminded me of the toughness and determination that characterized the American West.

Tombstone is more than simply a place; it's a trip through the heart of frontier life. The exhilaration of O.K. Corral, the seriousness of Boot Hill, and the bustling ambiance of the streets all work together to form a tapestry of history that is both compelling and enlightening.

As I went along Allen Street for the final time, I soaked in the sights and sounds, intending to take the essence of

Tombstone with me long after I departed. If you find yourself in Arizona, don't pass up the opportunity to visit this amazing town. Accept its stories, learn about its history, and allow yourself to get carried away by the spirit of the Wild West. You'll discover that Tombstone, the town too tough to die, will leave an everlasting impact on your heart, as it did mine.

CHAPTER 14

PAYSON

What To Do And Not To Do In The Heart Of Arizona

Payson, located in the heart of Arizona, felt like a hidden gem just waiting to be discovered. Surrounded by the beautiful views of the Mogollon Rim and the enormous Tonto National Forest, it's a location where the whispers of the pines blend with the fresh mountain air. My journey to Payson was packed with adventure, peace, and a great respect for nature's beauty.

Key Attractions

Payson is more than just a pretty town; it has a number of attractions that highlight the area's natural marvels and rich culture. Tonto Natural Bridge and Green Valley Park were two of the must-see attractions for me.

Tonto Natural Bridge: My journey through Payson began at Tonto Natural Bridge, a breathtaking natural phenomenon that had long attracted my interest. As I drove along the winding roads leading to the park, I was met with towering pine trees and the aroma of fresh earth—nature's perfume.

What To Do

Hike The Trails: Upon arrival, I immediately began exploring the trails. The trail to the natural bridge was well-kept and provided numerous views along the way. The short journey down to the bridge was a thrilling experience; each step drew me closer to this natural marvel. As I descended, the sound of running water from a nearby creek filled the air, providing a relaxing soundtrack to my quest. The anticipation grew as I approached the bridge, and when I finally saw it, I was completely taken aback. This huge stone arch, surrounded by bright vegetation, seemed something out of a fantasy story.

Explore The Visitor Center: After admiring the bridge, I visited the Visitor Center to learn about the area's history and geology through interesting displays. The courteous staff told us about the area fauna and recommended the best spots to see the natural bridge. I discovered that it is one of the world's largest natural bridges, a tribute to the power of nature over millennia. I picked up several pamphlets and maps, eager to learn more about this gorgeous region.

Photography Opportunities: I couldn't resist capturing the stunning sights. The interplay of light and shadows on the granite formations provided excellent photo opportunity. I spent my time, looking for the best perspectives to highlight the bridge's magnificence. If you enjoy photography as I do, bring your camera and a good lens to capture the splendor of this natural wonder.

What Not To Do

Remember To Stick To The Trails: Despite the beautiful surroundings, it's important to stay on designated paths. Going off-trail can harm the fragile ecology and disrupt the local fauna. Plus, there were signs warning of precipitous cliffs, and I had no intention of falling off a cliff! It is critical to respect the land and preserve its beauty for future visitors.

Don't Rush Your Visit: Some guests rushed to take pictures and move on to the next site. This place is worth your time and attention. Take a time to breathe in the pure mountain air and enjoy the calm surroundings. Allowing me to linger made the encounter significantly more rewarding.

Green Valley Park: After admiring the beauty of Tonto Natural Bridge, I made my way to Green Valley Park, a beautiful sanctuary in the middle of Payson. This park provides a perfect balance of recreational activities and tranquil surroundings, with something for everyone.

What To Do

Picnic By The Lake: The lovely lake, surrounded by lush green grass and tall trees, grabbed me from the moment I arrived. I found a nice area under a giant oak tree, unpacked my picnic, and ate a leisurely lunch while admiring the breathtaking sights. The gentle breeze rustled the leaves, generating a pleasant tune that made this moment feel like something out of a movie. I brought some local sweets from a neighboring bakery, which were a nice addition to my lunch.

Stroll The Walking Paths: After my picnic, I took a stroll along the lake's walking paths. The well-maintained trails were ideal for a leisurely stroll. I saw families fishing, children playing, and couples enjoying the peaceful surroundings. I stopped to chat with a few locals, who told me about their favorite areas in the park and the ideal times to go. Their friendliness and hospitality made me feel totally at home in this lovely neighborhood.

Visit The Playground And Sports Facilities: For families with children, the park has a great playground to keep them entertained. I paused to watch them climb and swing, their joy booming across the park. The park also has recreational amenities such as basketball and tennis courts, making it an ideal location for families or groups to congregate and engage in friendly rivalry.

What Not To Do

Don't Leave Trash Behind: While enjoying Green Valley Park, I saw some litter sprinkled throughout. It is critical to respect nature and leave no trace behind. I made a point of packing out everything I brought in, even picking up a few stray wrappers along the way. Keeping this beautiful park clean guarantees that it is preserved for future generations to enjoy.

Avoid Loud Noises: To maintain a pleasant atmosphere in the park, avoid making loud noises. This is not the place for loud music or disruptive conduct. Everyone gets to enjoy the beauty of nature in peace, and I tried to be mindful to my fellow parkgoers.

The Spirit Of Payson

As I reflected on my time in Payson, I concluded that the town's essence is woven throughout its scenery and the friendly nature of its residents. Visitors experience a palpable sense of community and a connection to the earth. Whether it was the thrill of discovering natural treasures or the simple joy of sharing a picnic in the park, the warmth of this one-of-a-kind location enhanced every moment.

What To Do

Engage With Local Culture: Engage with local culture by attending Payson's heritage-themed festivals and activities. I happened to be in town during the Payson Rodeo, which takes place every July and is one of Arizona's oldest rodeos. The thrill of the event brought people from all over, and I found myself cheering alongside other onlookers as cowboys demonstrated their abilities. Check the local calendar for activities that will allow you to thoroughly immerse yourself in the culture.

Explore The Shops And Local Eateries: Explore Payson's lovely downtown area, which features small shops and local eateries. I browsed the storefronts, discovering interesting goods and homemade crafts. I discovered a beautiful tiny café that provided delicious coffee and fresh pastries. While I was enjoying my sweets, the proprietor, a kind local, told me stories about the town's history. Engaging with the people is an excellent way to enhance your experience and learn about the community.

What Not To Do

Don't Overlook Small Businesses: Payson's heart is in its little businesses, rather than larger chain stores or eateries. Don't overlook them. These small businesses frequently provide one-of-a-kind products and a personal touch that larger firms cannot match. Make an effort to visit tiny boutiques and eat at family-run restaurants. You'll depart with more than simply souvenirs; you'll carry the spirit of Payson with you.

Avoid Rushing Departure: As my time in Payson came to a conclusion, I felt compelled to stay a little longer. I propose that you do not rush your departure. Take a beautiful drive around the neighboring mountains, or stop at one final viewpoint to take in the breathtaking views. Payson's serenity is worth enjoying, and the experiences you make here will last long after you leave.

Conclusion: Payson is a hidden gem in the middle of Arizona, with breathtaking scenery and a rich history. Every encounter here, from the breathtaking Tonto Natural Bridge to the tranquil Green Valley Park, serves as a reminder of nature's beauty and the friendliness of a community. As I packed my luggage and prepared to depart, I couldn't help but feel grateful for the memories I had made in this wonderful town.

If you find yourself in Arizona, be sure to include Payson on your itinerary. Accept the natural wonders, interact with the residents, and let yourself get swept away by the allure of this hidden jewel. Payson is more than just a destination; it is an experience that will leave an indelible mark on your heart, just as it did on mine.

CHAPTER 15

BISBEE

What To Do And Not To Do In This Historic Mining Town

As I reached Bisbee, a picturesque town nestled in the Mule Mountains of southwestern Arizona, I felt a rush of excitement. Bisbee, known for its rich mining heritage and active arts scene, has a distinct personality—a fusion of the past and present, with a story told on every street corner. Stepping into Bisbee is like opening the pages of a history book, but it's a living story with colors, noises, and characters.

Key Attractions

My top two attractions were the Copper Queen Mine and the Bisbee Mining & Historical Museum. Each location promised a better grasp of Bisbee's rich history as well as the opportunity to enjoy the town's distinct charm.

Copper Queen Mine: My first destination on the adventure was the Copper Queen Mine. It was once one of the world's richest copper mines, and now visitors can explore the depths of this historical gem.

What To Do

Take A Guided Tour: I I opted for a guided tour to learn about the mine's history. Our guide, a former miner with a sparkle in his eye, told us stories about the guys who worked down, facing the elements and working diligently to retrieve the rich copper. We descended into the mine's depths, wearing protective hats and carrying flashlights. The air was chilly and moist. The tunnels appeared to whisper stories from the past, and as we proceeded further, I could almost feel the weight of history pushing against us. I was amazed by the engineering accomplishments that enabled such a massive network of tunnels to be excavated from solid rock.

Learn About Mining Techniques: The excursion provided an opportunity to learn about mining techniques, in addition to exploration. I studied about several mining processes, starting with pickaxes and shovels and progressing to more advanced technology. Each method presented unique obstacles and accomplishments, demonstrating the inventiveness of individuals who worked there. I was especially interested by the stories of the workers who faced danger on a daily basis—this mine was more than simply a source of cash; it was a tribute to their tenacity and determination.

Experience the Miner's Life: The Stepping into a recreation of a miner's bunkhouse provided a peek into the living conditions of people who worked underground, making it a highlight for me. It was a stark reminder of the sacrifices made for the sake of development. I had a tremendous appreciation for the laborers who built this town and realized how much the mining sector influenced the lives of its residents.

What Not To Do

Don't Rush The Experience: Some travelers sped through the mine to complete their list. I discovered that the true beauty of the Copper Queen Mine rested in its stories and frightening yet interesting atmosphere. I took my time, soaking up every detail and allowed myself to be transported back in time. Don't be like those who miss the magic in the hurry; instead, take your time and appreciate this place's legacy.

Avoid Wearing Inappropriate Footwear: To navigate the mine's uneven terrain, it's important to wear strong shoes. I noticed a few people attempting the tour in flip-flops and sandals, apparently unprepared for the conditions. If you wish to visit the mine, wear comfortable, closed-toe shoes to securely navigate the uneven trails.

Bisbee Mining And Historical Museum: After the mine, I visited the Bisbee Mining and Historical Museum, which is a treasure trove of relics and displays that provide a vivid picture of the town's history.

What To Do

Explore The Exhibits: The museum is set in a historic structure and features exhibits highlighting Bisbee's history, including its establishment and mining boom. Each display told a tale, and I was particularly drawn to the images of miners and their families, their expressions full with hope and resolve. One exhibit highlighted the town's rich arts culture, and witnessing the works of local artists filled me with inspiration.

Participate In The Mining History Tour: I participated in a Mining History Tour that explored the influence of mining on the town. Our guide was informed and passionate, telling stories that brought history to life. She discussed the miners' unions and strikes that influenced labor rights in America. The spirit of perseverance resonated throughout the museum, and I felt strongly linked to the trials and accomplishments of others who had walked these same streets before me.

Visit The Gift Shop: Before leaving, I couldn't resist visiting the museum's gift shop, which showcased local craftsmen' work and interesting souvenirs. I purchased a beautifully handmade piece of jewelry fashioned from Bisbee turquoise, a gemstone with unique importance in the region. The shop also offered books about the town's history, which I couldn't pass up because I knew they'd be great souvenirs of my visit.

What Not To Do

Avoid Skipping Guided Tours: Some visitors choose to explore independently instead of taking guided tours. While I appreciate the ability to explore at my own leisure, I discovered that our guide's insights enhanced my trip significantly. The human experiences and historical backdrop provided additional layers of meaning that I would not have discovered otherwise. If you want to properly comprehend Bisbee's significance, don't miss the guided excursions.

Avoid Eating Immediately After The Museum: After learning so much about history, I felt drained and wanted some nourishment. However, I considered it prudent to take a minute to process what I had learnt before going out for a bite. Bisbee has a bustling food culture, and I wanted to be totally present during the experience. So I took a leisurely stroll into town to take in the sights and noises before sitting down to eat.

The Spirit Of Bisbee

As I wandered the twisting streets of Bisbee, I couldn't help but feel the town's heartbeat. It's a location where history and art collide, where old meets new, and where every turn offers something surprising.

What To Do

Wander The Historic District: Explore Bisbee's historic district, which offers a sensory feast. I became lost in the lively streets, where colorful buildings clung to the hillside, forming a patchwork of colors against the backdrop of the mountains. Each house has its own tale, and many have plaques outlining its past. I enjoyed meandering through the streets, admiring the exquisite architecture and the town's unique charm. The vibrant atmosphere and welcoming locals made me feel completely at home.

Enjoy The Local Art Scene: Bisbee boasts a vibrant artistic community. I discovered galleries displaying everything from traditional Western art to modern works that challenged the existing quo. One exhibition showcased local painters, and I was impressed by their dedication and inventiveness. I spoke with a few artists, learning about their influences and how Bisbee has influenced their artistic paths.

What Not To Do

Avoid Ignoring Local Events: Bisbee has a variety of events throughout the year, including art walks and music festivals. I wished I had researched the local calendar before my visit because it would have brought another dimension of excitement to my vacation. If you're planning a trip, look into what activities are taking place during your stay; it's a terrific way to become involved in the community and meet people.

Avoid Tourist Traps: Bisbee's true appeal rests in its authenticity, rather than the draw of souvenirs and tourist attractions. I encourage visiting local businesses and restaurants rather than purchasing mass-produced things. There are many unusual items to be discovered, and you will leave with more important memories.

Conclusion: My time in Bisbee was a discovery voyage, replete with rich history, breathtaking vistas, and a thriving arts community. From the depths of the Copper Queen Mine to the bustling streets of the historic area, each moment was an invitation to reconnect with the past while enjoying the present.

As I prepared to leave this wonderful town, I felt grateful for the experiences we had shared. Bisbee had knitted itself into the fabric of my journey, leaving me with tales to share and memories to treasure. If you're traveling through Arizona, make time to see Bisbee. It's a place that captures your heart, encouraging you to explore, study, and celebrate the spirit of a town with too much history to forget.

CHAPTER 16

APACHE JUNCTION

What To Do And Not To Do In The East Valley

Stepping into Apache Junction, I was struck by the obvious attraction of the Superstition Mountains in the distance, its craggy peaks carved against the sky like ancient sentinels. Nestled in Arizona's East Valley, this town serves as a gateway to breathtaking natural surroundings as well as a colorful past steeped in gold and mystery. As I navigated the sun-soaked streets, I knew I was in for an adventure full of stunning sights and fascinating anecdotes.

Key Attractions

My journey included two highlights: the Superstition Mountains and Lost Dutchman State Park. Each offered a distinct experience, full of beauty, difficulty, and the opportunity to connect with Arizona's rough soul.

Superstition Mountains: The Superstition Mountains are nothing short of breathtaking. Their name is rooted in folklore, since it is said to be the final resting place of the mythical Lost Dutchman Gold Mine. For decades, adventurers have been attracted to the mountains by stories of hidden wealth and terrifying apparitions.

What To Do

Hiking The Trails: I began my adventure at the Superstition Mountain Trailhead, ready to tackle one of the many trails that crisscross through this breathtaking area. I chose the Siphon Draw Trail, a reasonably difficult climb that leads to the Flatiron, the mountain's iconic top. The rise was both exciting and intimidating. As I went higher, the view changed from the dry desert bottom to sweeping panoramas of the valley below, highlighted by vivid desert vegetation. The cacti stood tall and strong, their arms reaching towards the sun, and the aroma of creosote filled the air, producing a heavy desert perfume.

Enjoy The Natural Beauty: I paused at the Flatiron to take in the panoramic view. The tremendous plummet to the valley below made my heart race, but the beauty was completely captivating. I took a moment to record the scene with my camera, knowing that the images would do little credit to the sensation of being there, surrounded by the expanse of nature. I inhaled the cool mountain air, allowing the tranquility to wash over me like a soothing salve.

Explore The Visitor Center: After my climb, I visited the Superstition Mountain Museum, which showcases artifacts and displays about the mountains and their inhabitants. The museum's exhibits include local flora and animals, mining history, and Native American relics from the region's original inhabitants. I was particularly interested by the legends of the early prospectors and their never-ending search for gold, which echoed the mountains' enduring fascination.

What Not To Do

Don't Underestimate The Terrain: I saw some hikers going out in flip-flops and without enough water. The trails, while stunning, can be misleading. I recommend wearing strong shoes and carrying plenty of water, especially during the hot months. The desert sun may be merciless, so staying hydrated is essential for having a safe and enjoyable experience.

Avoid Ignoring The Weather: I discovered that the weather in Apache Junction can shift suddenly. While my morning began with bright skies, storms can move very quickly. Always check the forecast before going out, and be prepared for changing weather. On the day of my visit, I wore layers, which proved to be a lifesaver when the temperature plummeted in the late afternoon.

Lost Dutchman State Park: After my mountain adventures, I was excited to visit Lost Dutchman State Park, a gorgeous oasis at the foot of the Superstitions. This park is named after the notorious gold mine and provides a variety of leisure options amidst breathtaking nature.

What To Do

Camping And Picnicking: I found the park's campgrounds relaxing and inviting. The locations were well-kept and surrounded by the natural beauty of the desert. I settled in for a picnic, savoring the flavors of fresh fruit and sandwiches while admiring the stunning vistas of the mountains above. There's something lovely about dining al fresco in the desert, with the warm sun on my skin and a nice breeze murmuring through the trees.

Photography And Wildlife Watching: I used my camera to record the park's splendor and observe wildlife. The scene was a photographer's dream, adorned with bright wildflowers and towering cactus. I also kept an eye out for local fauna, such as jackrabbits, lizards, and a variety of bird species flying around. The park is noted for its different ecosystems, and I felt fortunate to see creatures thrive in their natural environment.

Stargazing At Night: Nighttime stargazing revealed the park's full splendor. The absence of city lights allowed for fantastic stargazing. I lay back on a blanket and looked up at the huge expanse of glittering stars, feeling a strong connection to the universe. The Milky Way extended across the sky, a stunning sight that reminded me of my modest place in the universe.

What Not To Do

Don't Forget Your Camera: Don't miss the breathtaking views of Lost Dutchman State Park. Remember to bring your camera. I noticed some guests roaming around with no cameras or phones, missing out on capturing the beauty. Trust me—this is a destination you'll want to remember, so make sure to film your exploits.

Avoid Straying From Marked Routes: While it's tempting to investigate every nook and crevice, I learnt to stick to marked pathways. The desert may be harsh and unforgiving, and going off the main path might lead to problems. I stayed on authorized trails to safeguard both myself and the fragile desert habitat.

The Spirit Of Apache Junction

Beyond the breathtaking scenery, Apache Junction boasts a rich tapestry of history and culture. The town is rich in Old West traditions, and I was eager to discover its distinct character.

What To Do

Visit The Goldfield Ghost Town: Visit Goldfield Ghost Town, a reconstructed mining town located in Apache Junction that transports tourists back to the late 1800s. I explored the dusty streets, gazing into the old saloon and visiting the businesses selling homemade crafts and local goods. The smell of gunpowder permeated the air from live action displays, and I couldn't help but smile as cowboys performed their parts for the tourists. The atmosphere was bustling, and I felt as if I had stepped back into time.

Experience Local Events: Apache Junction features annual events such as rodeos, craft fairs, and music festivals. During my visit, I came across a local arts and crafts market where sellers showcased anything from handcrafted jewelry to exquisite paintings inspired by the surrounding surroundings. I engaged in conversations with local craftsmen, learning about their talents and the stories behind their products. The sense of togetherness was strong, and I departed feeling connected to the town and its inhabitants.

What Not To Do

Don't Rush Through the Town: Don't rush through Apache Junction; it's worth taking time to appreciate its charm. I saw a few tourists dashing by, eager to get to their next destination. I spent my time touring the local shops and conversing with the nice locals, who offered their experiences and recommendations. By slowing down, I discovered the town's heart and soul, learning that the journey is as important as the destination.

Avoid Ignoring Local History: The stories of Apache Junction and the Superstition Mountains are fascinating and colorful. I saw that several people were simply focused on the natural charms, ignoring the area's historical significance. Take the opportunity to read about the town's history, prospectors, and the legends surrounding the Lost Dutchman mine. Understanding the past enriches your experience and fosters a stronger connection to the location.

Conclusion: My time in Apache Junction was a wonderful combination of adventure, history, and natural beauty. The breathtaking Superstition Mountains served as a backdrop to my investigations, reminding me of the wild spirit of the West. From climbing the steep mountains to immersing myself in the local culture, every moment was an invitation to interact with this one-of-a-kind part of Arizona.

As I packed my luggage and prepared to depart, I felt grateful for the experiences I'd experienced. Apache Junction had knitted itself into the fabric of my travels, leaving me with stories to tell and memories to keep. If you find yourself in the East Valley, don't miss out on the attractions of Apache Junction. It's a location where adventure awaits around every corner, and the spirit of the Old West remains in the air, calling you to uncover its charm.

CHAPTER 17

JEROME

What To Do And Not To Do In Arizona's Ghost Town

As I approached Jerome, located high on the edge of Clyde Mountain, I couldn't suppress my excitement. Jerome, once a thriving copper mining town, is now an intriguing ghost town that provides a unique look into Arizona's rich history. The twisting route up to Jerome was as fascinating as the town itself, with breathtaking views of the Verde Valley below. I felt as if I was driving into a region where time had stopped, where the whispers of miners and dreamers lingered in the fresh mountain air.

Jerome isn't simply a ghost town; it's a living example of persistence and rebirth. While wandering its tiny alleyways lined with aged houses, I felt a strong link to the past—as if every brick and stone spoke stories of prosperity and failure, hard labor and heartbreak.

Key Attractions

During my visit, I focused on two major attractions: Jerome State Historic Park and the Gold King Mine. Each provided a unique viewpoint on the town's rich history, immersing me in the spirit of the Wild West.

Jerome State Historical Park: My first trip was Jerome State Historic Park, and I couldn't have had a better introduction to this incredible area. The park is built on the site of the former Jerome High School, a beautiful brick structure with a long history.

What To Do

Explore The Museum: The museum showcases artifacts and exhibits from Jerome's rich past. Old images of miners, families, and the town's thriving past piqued my interest. I walked through chambers packed with historic mining equipment, household goods, and even a recreated miner's cottage. Each piece told a tale, and I spent hours absorbing the intricacies. The intricate tapestry of lives lived here was captivating.

Enjoy The Scenic Views: After exploring the museum, I enjoyed the scenic views of the Verde Valley. The overlook near the park provided stunning panoramic views. The view of the wide valley below, with its lush foliage and winding river, was in stark contrast to the harsh mountains around me. I located a bench and took a time to ponder, watching the sun sink lower in the sky, casting a warm golden tone over everything.

Take A Guided Tour: I definitely recommend taking a guided tour. I got the opportunity to explore the park with a knowledgeable guide who offered fascinating stories and legends about Jerome's history. From stories of the mining boom to creepy legends of the town's ghostly inhabitants, I felt like I was walking into a live history book. The guide's enthusiasm for Jerome was contagious, and I hung onto every word.

What Not To Do

Don't Rush Your Visit: Some tourists rushed through the exhibits, looking at displays without really engaging. Jerome's heritage deserves to be cherished. Take your time, read the inscriptions, and absorb the stories. This location has a lot to teach you if you are prepared to listen.

Avoid The Heat Of The Day: If visiting during the summer, plan outside activities at cooler hours to avoid the heat. The sun can be fierce, and walking around the grounds in the midday heat can be difficult. I chose an early morning visit so that I could experience the park's magnificence before the sun rose.

Gold King Mine: After viewing the historic park, I drove to the nearby Gold King Mine. This one-of-a-kind attraction embodies Jerome's character by combining history, nostalgia, and whimsy.

What To Do

Explore The Grounds: The site's unique assortment of ancient mining equipment and buildings caught my eye right away. Rusty trucks, crumbling shacks, and mining ruins provided an interesting setting for exploration. I walked the grounds, photographing the interesting objects and marveling at human inventiveness in the past. It seemed like a treasure hunt, finding fragments of history concealed in plain sight.

Visit The Mining Museum: Inside the main structure, there is a small museum on mining history. The exhibitions included vintage images and tools used by miners in their search for gold and copper. I was particularly interested in the stories of the miners who risked everything to strike it rich. I also had the opportunity to speak with the owner, who told stories about his exploits in restoring the site and his passion for all things mining. His excitement for history was contagious, and I left with a renewed understanding for the sacrifices made by those before us.

Enjoy The Peculiar Attractions: Gold King Mine stands itself for its unusual art pieces, featuring sculptures built from scrap metal and other materials. I couldn't help but smile as I went among these strange constructions, each with its own narrative. I even stumbled onto a mini-zoo with a variety of animals, including goats and peacocks. It was a nice surprise that added to the attraction of the location.

What Not To Do

Don't Skip The Details: Don't speed through Gold King Mine. The magic is in the subtleties. Take the time to read the information plaques and enjoy the stories behind the items. I found satisfaction in the smallest things—a rusted spade, a faded snapshot, a strange statue—each telling a part of Jerome's tale.

Avoid Touching Unsecured Items: During my exploration, I observed guests recklessly handling objects that were plainly not meant to be touched. While it may be tempting to touch with historical relics, keep in mind that many are fragile and irreplaceable. Respect the history and the work of people who care for these sites. I took great precautions to follow the requirements, insuring the longevity of this living museum.

The Spirit Of Jerome

As I walked through the town, I couldn't help but feel Jerome's spirit—history woven into the very fabric of the buildings and the stories of its citizens. Although the town is well-known for its ghosts, it also thrives on art, culture, and a sense of community.

What To Do

Check Out Local Art Galleries: Visit Jerome's art galleries to see local artists' work. I strolled inside a few galleries, each with a distinct piece inspired by the town's surroundings and history. The artists poured their hearts and souls into their work, and I was charmed by their devotion. I departed with a modest piece of art that I treasure as a remembrance of my stay in Jerome.

Experience Local Events: Visit Jerome during one of its festivals to really immerse yourself in the local culture. From art walks to live music events, the town exudes a lively vibe that is infectious. I happened to be in town for the Jerome Historic Home and Building Tour, which allowed me to explore the town's architecture and hear about preservation efforts. Interacting with residents at these events strengthened my connection to the community and its history.

What Not To Do

Don't Ignore The Local Cuisine: Don't miss out on the local cuisine in Jerome, a small town with many dining alternatives that reflect its unique character. I made sure to taste some local delicacies, including The Haunted Hamburger, a strange establishment with great burgers and a vibrant ambiance. Some visitors may neglect dining options, but I believe that food is an important element of the vacation experience. The flavors of Jerome were as remarkable as the vistas.

Avoid The Off-Season If Possible: If possible, visit Jerome during peak tourist season to really enjoy the town's vibrant atmosphere. During my vacation, I discovered that the local events and activities enhanced my enjoyment of the trip. If feasible, plan your vacation for spring or fall, when the weather is nice and the town is bustling.

Conclusion: My experience in Jerome was nothing short of wonderful. As I wandered its streets, I felt a deep connection to the past and a renewed appreciation for the tenacity of individuals who called this town home. More than just a ghost town, Jerome celebrates history, creativity, and community.

As I prepared to depart, I took one final look at the stunning landscapes and lovely neighborhoods, thankful for the experiences I had gained. Jerome taught me that every ghost town has a heartbeat, and if you listen carefully, you may hear its stories whispering through the ages. So, if you find yourself on the meandering route to this beautiful location, enjoy the adventure. Allow Jerome's spirit to grip you and inspire you to tell your own stories long after you've left its ghostly beauty behind.

CHAPTER 18

SHOW LOW

What To Do And Not To Do In The White Mountains

Show Low, located in Arizona's magnificent White Mountains, is a hidden gem that travelers consider to be a well-kept secret. As I entered this picturesque village, the aroma of pine and cold mountain air surrounded me, renewing my spirit after the dry desert heat. Show Low, known for its breathtaking natural beauty, is an ideal vacation for outdoor enthusiasts, families, and anybody wishing to immerse themselves in nature. I was excited to see what this small town had to offer, armed with a sense of adventure and a quest for exploration.

Key Attractions

During my vacation, I concentrated on two major attractions: Show Low Lake and the Fool Hollow Lake Recreation Area. Both locations encapsulated the essence of Show Low, providing limitless chances for relaxation and enjoyment amidst stunning nature.

Show Low Lake: My first stop was Show Low Lake, a magnificent body of water located in the middle of the White Mountains. The journey to the lake was beautiful, with tall pines surrounding the road and wildflowers painting the landscape in vivid colors. As I reached the lake, I could feel the serenity pour over me, promising a day of relaxation and discovery.

What To Do

Fishing And Boating: Upon arrival, I was surprised by a calm lake surrounded by thick trees and steep mountains, ideal for fishing and boating. Fishing is a popular hobby here, and I watched many anglers casting their lines into the lake in the hopes of catching a trout or two. I decided to rent a small boat and see the lake from a fresh perspective. As I flew across the surface, the smooth lapping of water on the hull, combined with distant bird cries, created a natural symphony. The fresh breeze and breathtaking vistas of the mountains were simply divine, making me feel as if I had discovered my own personal slice of paradise.

Hiking And Biking: After a relaxing boat ride, I traded my oars for hiking boots. Show Low Lake is surrounded by numerous trails that offer opportunities for hikers of all skill levels. I chose a moderate track that ringed the lake, guiding me through scented trees and providing breathtaking views of the water. Along the way, I noticed a family of deer gently moving through the trees. Hiking in this tranquil setting was energizing, and I couldn't help but stop regularly to take photos and admire the gorgeous view.

Picnicking: I found many picnic places along the lake, all with tables and grills. After working up an appetite, I located the ideal location under a towering tree to put out my picnic blanket. I sipped my lunch while enjoying in the tranquil ambiance, looking out at the glistening lake and rustling branches overhead. There's something amazing about eating outdoors, surrounded by nature; it's a memory I'll cherish.

What Not To Do

Don't Forget Your Sunscreen: Remember to bring sunscreen as the sun may be harsh even in milder mountain climates. I made the mistake of neglecting to apply sunscreen before going to the lake, and I ended up with an unpleasant sunburn. Remember to protect your skin, especially on cloudy days; you'll thank yourself later.

Avoid Littering: While admiring the beauty of Show Low Lake, I spotted some trash left behind by inconsiderate visitors. I made a point of packing out everything I brought in, and I encourage everyone to do the same. Keeping our natural areas clean is critical to preserving their beauty for future generations. It's also an easy method to demonstrate environmental stewardship.

Fool Hollow Lake Recreation Area: My next stop was Fool Hollow Lake Recreation Area, which was only a short drive from Show Low Lake. This large park provides a range of leisure opportunities against a magnificent backdrop of pine-covered hills and tranquil lakes.

What To Do

Camping: I was impressed by the natural beauty of Fool Hollow Lake. The recreation area has well-maintained campsites where guests can immerse themselves in nature. I decided to set up a tent for the night, anxious to experience the serenity of sleeping under the stars. The sound of the wind through the trees and the smooth rippling of the lake provided a relaxing lullaby, making it easy to fall asleep. Waking up to see the sunrise spread a golden glow across the lake was an unforgettable experience.

Swimming And Water Sports: Fool Hollow Lake is ideal for cooling off in the summer heat. I joined families splashing in the water, which was a welcome respite from the warmer weather. Kayaking and paddleboarding are also popular pastimes, and I couldn't pass up hiring a kayak for a relaxing paddle. I glided across the lake, admiring the reflections of the surrounding trees dancing on the water's surface, feeling completely at ease.

Wildlife Watching: Nature lovers will enjoy the abundance of species in the region surrounding Fool Hollow Lake. As I explored the lake's trails, I was fortunate to see a variety of species, including bald eagles and beautiful songbirds. I also kept an eye out for rabbits and other animals that call this location home. Birdwatching rapidly became one of my favorite activities during my stay.

What Not To Do

Don't Overlook Safety Precautions: When swimming or kayaking in the lake, it's important to follow safety precautions. Wearing a life jacket is essential, especially for beginners or those going out alone. It's better to be safe than sorry. I also kept an eye on the weather forecast, as storms may come in fast in the highlands. I recommend checking the weather before venturing out for a day of fun.

Avoid Playing Loud Music: Avoid playing loud music in quiet areas. I noticed some groups blasting loud music, which took away from the natural beauty around us. Instead, I chose peaceful discussions and the sounds of nature to enhance the whole experience.

The Charm Of Show Low

Beyond its lakes and recreational activities, Show Low has a distinct appeal that entices visitors to explore its small-town ambiance. The town's heart is brimming with friendly inhabitants, one-of-a-kind businesses, and delectable restaurants that enhance the overall experience.

What To Do

Visit The Local Shops: I couldn't resist exploring downtown Show Low. The main street is dotted with charming stores selling local art, homemade crafts, and one-of-a-kind souvenirs. I spent hours traveling from store to store, conversing with shop owners who were eager to share their experiences. I discovered a stunning hand-painted ceramic item that now has a particular place in my home, reminding me of my time in Show Low.

Dine At Local Restaurants: After an adventurous day, I enjoyed a lunch at The Red Onion, a local restaurant. This quaint eatery is well-known for its courteous service and great comfort cuisine. I had a big bowl of homemade chili and cornbread, loving each bite while taking in the pleasant atmosphere. The residents' recommendations for their favorite foods really enhanced the experience, and I departed feeling fulfilled and grateful for the amazing gastronomic options.

What Not To Do

Don't Rush Your Visit: To fully experience Show Low's laid-back environment, don't rush your visit. Take your time. I noticed a few visitors racing through town, oblivious to the community's charm and kindness. Slow down, talk to people, and take in the atmosphere. By fully immersing yourself in the town, you will generate more significant memories.

Don't Miss Seasonal Activities: Take advantage of local activities throughout your visit. I was fortunate to stumble onto a summer event that had local craftsmen, food booths, and live music. The bustling atmosphere drew the community together, and I liked socializing with both residents and fellow travelers. Participating in these events provided another dimension of enjoyment to my trip.

Conclusion: My visit to Show Low was a welcome respite from the hustle and bustle of everyday life. From the peaceful shores of Show Low Lake to the vivid trails of Fool Hollow Lake, every moment spent in the White Mountains felt like a gift. The area provides the perfect balance of outdoor sports and small-town charm, making it a wonderful getaway for anybody wishing to unwind and reconnect with nature.

As I prepared to leave this wonderful town, I felt grateful for the experiences I'd had. Show Low showed me the value of taking a break from the hustle and bustle of daily life to enjoy the beauty of nature. The experiences I made here, from the calm lapping of lake waves to the laughs shared with locals, will stick with me long after I go. If you're planning a trip to the White Mountains, I heartily recommend that you experience Show Low's charm. It's a location where adventure awaits, and the spirit of community surrounds you like a warm embrace.

CHAPTER 19

GLOBE

What To Do And Not To Do In The Heart Of The Copper Country

Globe, nestled among Arizona's Rocky Mountains and desert landscapes, is a community steeped in history and character. When I came, I felt an immediate connection to the past. Globe, once a thriving mining town, has evolved into a charming destination that honors its history while embracing the present. Globe is a mesmerizing visit for any traveler, because to its stunning environment, fascinating historical landmarks, and dynamic community.

Key Attractions

During my stay, I concentrated on two notable sites: Besh-Ba-Gowah Archaeological Park and the Globe Historic District. Each area not only highlights Globe's distinct history, but also provides insight into the lives of those who came before us.

Besh-Ba-Gowah Archaeological Park: My journey began in Besh-Ba-Gowah Archaeological Park, an awe-inspiring site that honors the ancient Salado people who lived in this region. As I stepped through the door, I could feel the weight of history, met by the sight of reconstructed ruins that had withstood the test of time.

What To Do

Explore The Ruins: As I walked through the park, I was impressed by the exquisite stonework and creative design of the structures. The main ruin, a multi-story adobe edifice, was once a bustling center for the Salado community. I was charmed by the arrangement, picturing families gathering in the pleasant shade and children's laughter ringing through the halls. The park is well-preserved, with interpretative plaques explaining the significance of the numerous structures. It felt like I was moving back in time, interacting with a civilization that thrived in this desert region centuries before.

Visit The Museum: The Besh-Ba-Gowah Museum, located near the ruins, provided valuable insight into the area's history. The museum displays amazing artifacts, pottery, and tools from the Salado culture. I spent hours examining the exhibitions, captivated by the stories they conveyed. A competent curator was on hand to answer questions and provide insights. Engaging with the artifacts and learning about the Salado people's daily life made me appreciate their tenacity and ingenuity.

Take A Guided Tour: I definitely recommend taking a guided tour if available. Our group was led by a local historian who told stories of the Salado people's customs, connection to the land, and eventual decline. Listening to these stories while standing in the same places they lived was a rewarding experience. The guide's enthusiasm for preserving this history was contagious, increasing my attachment to the location.

What Not To Do

Don't Rush Your Visit: Don't rush your visit to Besh-Ba-Gowah. It merits your whole attention. I had planned to spend only an hour, but I became utterly captivated in the park. I recommend that you set aside plenty of time to take in the history and atmosphere. There is no need to rush; instead, allow yourself to explore, reflect, and thoroughly experience the sight.

Avoid Straying Off Paths: To enjoy the park, stay on specified routes and avoid wandering off. The archaeological ruins are sensitive, and walking off can result in inadvertent damage. Respecting the location helps to preserve its integrity while also honoring the legacy of individuals who lived there.

Globe Historic District: After immersing myself in the ancient past at Besh-Ba-Gowah, I headed to the Globe Historic District. This region is a treasure mine of architectural marvels and active local culture, reflecting the town's rich mining history.

What To Do

Stroll The Streets: Walking through the historic district, I was captivated by the well-preserved structures that tell stories of bygone eras. From the stately Victorian residences to the solid brick businesses, each structure adds to the charm of Globe. I spent my time wandering, gazing into shop windows and appreciating vintage craftsmanship. The community's dedication to maintaining its history is clear, and it's encouraging to witness how the past influences the present.

Visit Local Businesses: The main street features a variety of interesting boutiques and artisan businesses. The Copper Hen, a particularly wonderful boutique, drew my attention. This beautiful business sold locally manufactured goods ranging from handmade jewelry to artisanal soaps. I started up a chat with the owner, who told me the stories behind her works. Supporting local craftsmen not only improves the shopping experience, but also builds a strong feeling of community in Globe.

Enjoy A Meal At A Historic Eatery: After touring, I went to a local restaurant for some typical Arizona cuisine. I found myself in The Silver King Steakhouse, a historic restaurant that has been serving wonderful food for decades. The welcoming atmosphere and kind staff made me feel completely at home. I had a delicious steak served with seasonal vegetables while admiring the restaurant's rustic atmosphere. Sharing stories with other diners improved the overall experience; there's something wonderful about connecting with others over a shared dinner.

What Not To Do

Don't Miss The Historic Markers: As I walked through the district, I spotted various historical markers highlighting major events and personalities from Globe's past. It's easy to miss these jewels in the midst of exploration, but I encourage taking the time to read them. Each marker adds richness to the experience by contextualizing the structures and neighborhoods.

Avoid Taking Photos Without Permission: While documenting memories is important, some store owners prefer not to have their enterprises shot. It's usually courteous to ask before taking pictures, especially at smaller, family-owned businesses. This regard for local culture promotes goodwill and assures beneficial interactions with the community.

The Heart Of Copper Country

Globe is commonly referred to as the "Heart of Copper Country," and with good cause. The town's identity is molded by its mining heritage, and vestiges of that era may be found throughout daily life. As I explored, I learned how the past continues to impact the present.

What To Do

Visit The Old Dominion Mine Park: Explore Globe's mining past at the Old Dominion Mine Park, located just a short drive from the historic district. I examined the remains of the old mine, amazed at the scale of operations that formerly occurred. The park's interpretive displays explain the mining process and its impact on the town. Standing among the ruins, I was impressed by the miners' hard work and perseverance in these terrible conditions. The views of the surrounding mountains enhanced the experience, serving as a sobering reminder of the tenacity required to exist in such an environment.

Engage With Local History: Visit the Gila County Historical Museum to learn about the history of Globe and the surrounding area. I discovered interesting exhibits and knowledgeable staff who shared a plethora of information. The museum's collection contains mining relics, pictures, and deeply moving personal stories. Spending time here helped me comprehend Globe's role in Arizona's history and made me respect the community's efforts to preserve its heritage.

What Not To Do

Don't Neglect To Check Local Events: Check out local events in Globe that celebrate local history, art, and music, as the community values its culture. I stumbled into a vibrant street market with local merchants, live music, and delectable cuisine. The atmosphere during the event was amazing, and I met many pleasant residents ready to share their stories. Keep an eye on local calendars or ask visitor centers about future events.

Avoid Driving Too Fast Around Town: Globe's streets are not meant for rushing. The town's attractiveness can best be savored at a slow pace. Furthermore, traveling too rapidly can cause you to miss the charming features that distinguish Globe, such as murals painted on the sides of buildings and warm waves from inhabitants.

Conclusion: My time in Globe was a lovely exploration of history, culture, and community. Exploring the ancient remains of Besh-Ba-Gowah and meandering around the old area, I felt a strong connection to the town and its rich tapestry of stories. The kindness of the residents and the beauty of the surroundings instilled a sense of belonging in me, making me reluctant to go.

Globe epitomizes the spirit of Arizona's Copper Country, allowing tourists to explore the history while enjoying the present. The experiences I had—fishing for information at the archeological park, eating local cuisine, and roaming the picturesque streets—reminded me of the value of embracing history and community. As I drove away, I carried not only memories, but also a renewed appreciation for the heart and spirit of this magnificent community. If you find yourself in Arizona, don't pass on Globe; it is a destination that will enrich your travels and leave you wanting more.

CHAPTER 20

SAFETY TIPS FOR ARIZONA

Things To Avoid For A Safer Experience

Having spent a significant amount of time traveling across Arizona, I've gained some helpful insights about remaining safe while enjoying the beautiful beauty of this southwestern treasure. From the bright deserts to the gorgeous mountains, Arizona offers adventures that are both thrilling and challenging. In this chapter, I'll share my experiences and vital safety guidelines to ensure that your vacation is both pleasurable and safe.

Understanding The Environment

Arizona is known for its breathtaking vistas, yet its natural beauty frequently masks the hazards of its surroundings. My first hike in the Superstition Mountains left me fascinated by the rocky terrain and vivid wildflowers. However, it didn't take long for me to discover that the same beauty could lead to dangerous situations if I wasn't cautious.

What To Avoid

Ignoring Weather Warnings: The Arizona climate is unpredictable. I discovered this the hard way when hiking in the summer. The temperature can climb, often topping 100°F (38°C), and failing to check the weather before leaving might result in exhaustion or heat-related ailments. Before engaging in any outside activity, always consult the local forecast. Rainstorms can sometimes strike quickly, particularly during the monsoon season, resulting in flash floods. If you see heavy clouds forming, it's time to reconsider your plans and seek safer ground.

Underestimating Terrain: While routes may appear simple on a map, the reality can be quite different. I once took a "moderate" hike and quickly found myself laboring with high inclines and uneven roads. Always investigate the routes ahead of time and take into account your fitness level. If a trail is labeled as strenuous, it is necessary to prepare thoroughly or choose another route. I've discovered that beginning with well-traveled pathways, such as those in Sedona, might help you assess your hiking abilities before moving into more difficult locations.

What To Do

Hydrate: In Arizona, it's crucial to stay hydrated. On longer excursions, I always bring at least a gallon of water and consume it regularly to stay hydrated. It's easy to miss this until it's too late. In the desert heat, dehydration can occur quickly. A good trick I learned was to set reminders on my phone to take a sip every 20 minutes. This simple habit made a huge difference on my hikes.

Wear Appropriate Gear: I learnt to invest in high-quality, weather-resistant gear. Sturdy hiking boots are essential; they provide the ankle support I require when navigating rocky terrains. Lightweight, moisture-wicking clothing keeps me cool, while a wide-brimmed hat protects me from the sun. Sunscreen is essential, even on gloomy days, because UV rays can be fairly potent.

Wildlife Encounters

Arizona's various ecosystems are home to a wide range of species, including stately deer and elusive mountain lions. On one unforgettable occasion, while camping in Tonto National Forest, I spotted a family of javelinas. It was a beautiful experience, but it also served as a lesson of how to approach wildlife responsibly.

What To Avoid

Getting Too Close To Wildlife: Getting too close to wildlife can be dangerous for both humans and the animals. I've seen tourists get too close to deer or coyotes for the ideal shot, but wildlife can react unexpectedly when frightened. Admire from a distance and utilize a zoom lens to record those recollections.

Leaving Food Out: While camping, I discovered that leaving food alone can invite unpleasant guests. During one trip, I awakened to discover my goodies stolen by a cunning raccoon. Now, I always keep food in sealed containers and use bear-proof lockers when they're available. It is also advisable to remove all waste to avoid attracting wildlife.

What To Do

Learn About Local Species: Before visiting a new location, it's important to learn about the local animals. Knowing which animals are common can help me determine what to look for—and avoid. Understanding rattlesnake warning signs, for example, can help you stay safe on walks. When I hear a rattle, I know to slowly back away and give the snake space. The same goes for scorpions and spiders; learning their routines can help you avoid them.

Stay Calm In Wildlife Encounters: If you encounter wildlife unexpectedly, my suggestion is to remain calm. For example, if you come across a rattlesnake on the trail, I learnt to freeze briefly and let it to crawl away before continuing. Animals are often as wary of humans as we are of them. You can secure your own and others' safety by maintaining calm and gradually backing away.

Sun Exposure And Heat: The Arizona sun may be a blessing as well as a punishment. While it provides breathtaking views and pleasant weather, it can also result in serious burns or heatstroke if you are not careful.

What To Avoid

Neglecting Sun Protection: Sun protection is crucial for healthy skin. On my first day without sunscreen, I experienced the terrible lesson of sunburns. I now use a broad-spectrum sunscreen with at least SPF 30 and reapply every couple of hours, especially if I'm sweating. Don't forget about your ears and the back of your neck—they're commonly forgotten!

Overexerting Yourself In The Heat: I miscalculated the impact of heat on my stamina when trekking in Arizona. I learned to listen to my body and pace myself, particularly on noon treks. If I became warm or tired, I would rest in shaded spots and water adequately before resuming.

What To Do

Plan Outdoor Activities Wisely: In Arizona, the optimal times for outdoor activities are in the morning and evening. The temperatures are lower, and the sun is less harsh, resulting in a far more enjoyable experience. Plus, the desert sunsets are breathtaking—definitely worth the early start!

Keep A First-Aid Kit Handy: Always keep a modest first-aid kit with you when exploring, as accidents can happen anywhere. I add antiseptic wipes, adhesive bandages, pain relievers, and allergy meds. This way, I'm ready for small scrapes and unforeseen allergies, allowing me to enjoy my vacation.

Vehicle Safety

Traveling in Arizona frequently includes large expanses of open road. While driving through breathtaking scenery is part of the appeal, I've experienced obstacles that have taught me the value of vehicle safety.

What To Avoid

Neglecting Vehicle Maintenance: Prior to a long travel, I always verify my vehicle is in good shape. I acquired this lesson after getting a flat tire on an isolated stretch of highway in Southern Arizona. Routine checks for oil levels, tire pressure, and brakes are critical. It is also a good idea to make sure your spare tire is in good condition and that you have the tools to change it if necessary.

Ignoring Road Conditions: Arizona's road conditions can fluctuate significantly, especially during the rainy season. I've seen mudslides and debris on remote roads. Always check for road closures or warnings before leaving, especially if you intend to drive on less-traveled routes.

What To Do

Carry An Emergency Kit: I always carry an emergency kit with water, snacks, a flashlight, blankets, and a first-aid kit. Having these materials on hand might be quite beneficial in the event of unforeseen delays or car problems. I was once delayed in a rural region due to a sudden thunderstorm and was thankful to have food on hand.

Stay Informed About Your Path: I always familiarize myself with my path. GPS is useful, but it can occasionally lead you astray, particularly in mountainous places. Having a physical map as a backup has rescued me multiple times. There's nothing like old-fashioned navigation to help you connect with the terrain.

Respecting Local Customs And Laws

Arizona boasts a varied range of cultures and traditions. It is critical to follow local customs, particularly while visiting Native American reserves and towns.

What To Avoid

Disregarding Cultural Signage: When visiting areas like Montezuma Castle National Monument, it's important to respect sacred sites and not disregard cultural signs. Ignoring these notices might be extremely disrespectful to the indigenous tribes. I always make a point of reading and following any established guidelines.

Taking Photos Without Permission: Some cultural places forbid photography. Always get permission before taking images, especially if they involve individuals or sensitive sites. Respect for these customs promotes goodwill and understanding between visitors and the local population.

What To Do

Engage With Local Cultures: Understanding local customs and traditions enhances the trip experience. Whether it's attending a cultural event or simply conversing with a local artist, appreciating the diversity of Arizona's cultures enriches my journey.

Support Local Businesses: I prioritize supporting locally owned companies and artists. Buying homemade items or dining at local restaurants not only enhances my experience, but also benefits the community. Furthermore, the tales behind these objects are frequently as engaging as the items themselves.

Conclusion: Navigating the wonders of Arizona is a journey full of beauty, excitement, and potential problems. My experiences taught me the value of safety and respect for the environment as well as the people that live in this state. Understanding the landscape, being cautious of wildlife, preparing for the sun, ensuring vehicle safety, and respecting local customs have allowed me to explore with confidence.

With the proper preparation and a respectful mindset, you, too, can appreciate Arizona's breathtaking scenery and rich cultures. Enjoy the experience, remain safe, and enjoy the memories you make along the way. Arizona is a place where the spirit of adventure thrives, and with these suggestions in your pocket, you'll be ready to discover all of its treasures.

CHAPTER 21

CULTURAL SENSITIVITY

What Not To Do When Interacting With Local Communities

Traveling through Arizona was nothing short of transformative for me. This state, with its stunning scenery and rich cultural tapestry, provides a unique opportunity to interact with a wide range of local populations. However, my voyage has taught me that such encounters come with the duty of knowing and respecting the cultures, traditions, and histories of individuals who live on this country. In this chapter, I'll discuss my own experiences and insights for handling cultural sensitivity in Arizona, with a focus on what not to do while interacting with local people.

Understanding Arizona's Diverse Culture

Arizona has a diverse cultural landscape, with a sizable Native American population as well as influences from Hispanic, Anglo, and other groups. Each tribe has distinct customs and histories that add to the state's colorful identity. When I first arrived in Arizona, I was eager to immerse myself in its diversity, but I immediately realized that respect and understanding were essential.

What Not To Do

Assume Homogeneity: I mistakenly assumed that all Native American tribes have similar practices and beliefs. During my journey to the Navajo Nation, I quickly discovered how varied each tribe is, with its own languages, rituals, and history. Making broad generalizations can lead to misunderstandings or, worse, hurt those I attempted to connect with. I learnt to approach each group with an open mind, ready to respect their distinct viewpoints.

Disregard Historical Context: While touring sites like Chaco Canyon, I was attracted by the old remains and traditions of the Pueblo people, disregarding historical context. However, I found that some tourists treated history as mere amusement. This approach can be deeply disrespectful, given many local groups' tragic histories of colonization, relocation, and cultural degradation. I considered it critical to educate oneself about the historical settings of the sites I visited in order to honor those who came before me.

What To Do

Research Before Visiting: I Before traveling, I always conduct research on local communities and histories. Understanding the significance of cultural monuments like Monument Valley enhanced my experience and enabled me to have meaningful talks with local guides. I recall conversing with a Navajo guide who expressed his thoughts on the land and its meaning, which transformed my appreciation for the environment into something much more profound.

Listen Actively: I discovered the importance of active listening during interactions with local community people. I approached talks with interest, giving others opportunity to tell their story. While touring the Hopi Reservation, I chatted with a local artisan who revealed the rich symbolism of her pottery. This exchange not only helped me better understand Hopi culture, but it also developed a true bond.

Respecting Traditions And Customs

During my travels, I experienced a variety of cultures and traditions that, while fascinating, demanded careful thought and respect.

What Not To Do

Disregard Sacred Sites: My urge to explore led me to disregard their sacred value. For example, when I visited the Chapel of the Holy Cross in Sedona, I was tempted to shoot random photos, forgetting that this area has spiritual significance for many people. The reactions of locals reminded me that not all locations are suitable for casual investigation; some are genuinely sacred and should be handled with respect.

Interrupt Rituals Or Ceremonies: While visiting a reserve, I noticed an intriguing ceremony and automatically reached for my camera. Fortunately, I halted. Photographs can be obtrusive during religious rites, and interrupting such moments is extremely disrespectful. I discovered that being a courteous observer often speaks louder than any shot I could capture.

What To Do

Ask For Permission: To ensure acceptable photography, always seek permission first. Most community members appreciate the gift and are often eager to share their culture. This technique not only demonstrates respect but also allows for deeper connections. During a visit to a Zuni Pueblo festival, I was encouraged to photograph their traditional dances after obtaining permission, which enhanced my experience and allowed me to capture the essence of the event in a respectful manner.

Participate Mindfully: Participating mindfully in local customs can be a meaningful way to connect with the community. But I learnt to do so with humility and respect. For example, during a Dia de los Muertos celebration in Tucson, I helped build an ofrenda (offering altar), but I made sure to grasp its significance and sought advice from locals on how to properly honor the tradition. This approach not only improved my experience, but it also increased my appreciation for the culture.

Engaging With Local Economies

Supporting local businesses is an important aspect of ethical travel. However, I've found that how I interact with local companies and artists requires careful consideration.

What Not To Do

Bargain Aggressively: When I first met local craftspeople in markets, I instinctively tried to bargain pricing. I rapidly found that many artists set rates based on their time, effort, and the cultural relevance of their work. Haggling over prices might be perceived as rude, lowering the value of their craftsmanship. I soon realized that appreciating the creativity frequently entailed paying their asking rates.

Shop Only At Chain Stores: When traveling, it can be tempting to shop only at familiar chain stores, without considering the influence on local economies. In locations like Bisbee, I found that buying at small stores not only benefits the community but also provides opportunities for unusual discoveries. The excitement of discovering handcrafted jewelry or locally sourced art far exceeds anything I could find in a big-box retailer.

What To Do

Support Local Artisans: I actively sought out local artists and vendors on my travels. I remember going to an art gallery in Santa Fe and meeting a painter who told me about his trip and motivation. Purchasing a piece of his work not only helped him, but also served as a concrete remembrance of the culture and tales I had encountered.

Learn The Stories Behind The Art: Engage with local craftsmen to learn about their work and uncover the stories behind each piece of art. At a Hopi pottery studio, I learnt the significance of each pattern and technique. This connection made my purchase more significant, and I departed with a great respect for the artistry behind the work.

Interact With Indigenous Communities

Many locations in Arizona are home to Indigenous tribes, and connecting with them necessitates a sophisticated awareness of their specific situations.

What Not To Do

Assume A Monolithic Experience: I mistakenly assumed that all Indigenous people had comparable experiences. Each community faces unique challenges and capabilities, and seeing them as a single group reduces their rich diversity. During a journey to Tuba City, I discovered that the Navajo and Hopi tribes have different histories and perspectives. Engaging with each group individually allowed me to completely grasp their unique characteristics.

Make Assumptions Based On Stereotypes: When making assumptions based on stereotypes, it's important to recognize that they may not accurately represent the intricacies of individuals within a group. Instead of making assumptions about people's behaviors or views, I concentrated on engaging them directly and allowing them to develop their own identities.

What To Do

Acknowledge Historical Contexts: Recognizing the historical background of Indigenous communities in Arizona was essential for me. Many people continue to struggle as a result of colonization, and realizing this history has allowed me to approach conversations with respect and compassion. Learning about events like the Navajo people's Long Walk made me realize how resilient and strong these communities are.

Engage In Cultural interchange: Genuine cultural interchange promotes mutual respect and understanding. I recall attending a Navajo weaving lesson and participating in a workshop given by an accomplished weaver. Not only did I learn a useful skill, but I also received understanding into the significance of weaving in Navajo society. Sharing knowledge fosters a sense of reciprocity, benefiting both parties.

Conclusion: Exploring Arizona's diverse landscapes and populations requires cultural sensitivity. My travel has taught me the value of respecting local customs, communicating thoughtfully with those I meet, and appreciating the history that shape their identities. Through attentive listening, respectful engagement, and a commitment to understanding, I've discovered that travel is more than just seeing new locations; it's about connecting with the heart of a community.

As you start on your own Arizona experiences, keep in mind that your presence might have a long-term impact. Approach each interaction with humility and curiosity, and you'll find that the richness of the local cultures will repay you tenfold. Finally, travel is about bridging gaps and increasing understanding, and with each polite encounter, we create a richer tapestry of shared human experience. So let us honor the stories of everyone we meet, and by doing so, we will enhance our own journeys.

CHAPTER 22

ENVIRONMENTAL CONSIDERATIONS

What To Do And Not To Do To Protect Arizona's Natural Beauty

As a tourist charmed by Arizona's rough beauty, I am constantly amazed by its breathtaking landscapes, from the red rocks of Sedona to the broad deserts of Tucson and the beautiful peaks of the San Francisco Mountains. Each visit fills me with wonder, but it also delivers a sobering reality of my role as a tourist. Protecting Arizona's natural beauty is both a duty and a privilege. In this chapter, I'd want to give my opinions on how to manage this wonderful ecosystem with respect and care, focusing on what to do and what not to do so that future generations can enjoy the beauty of this place.

Understanding Arizona's Environment

Before heading into Arizona's vast wilderness, I took some time to learn about the state's unique ecological tapestry. Arizona's environment is diverse, including deserts, mountains, canyons, and forests. It is a biodiverse region, home to numerous plant and animal species. I discovered that being conscious of this diversity is critical in my efforts to protect it.

What Not To Do

Avoid Disregarding Local Ecosystems: During my travels, I realized the need of preserving the delicate balance of local ecosystems. For example, while trekking in Saguaro National Park, I was struck by the towering cacti that have become symbols of the American Southwest. However, I saw guests trampling the delicate desert plants, ignorant to the damage they were causing. Every footprint in the delicate desert soil has an impact, and ignoring this fact can endanger the same ecosystems that attract us to this magnificent place.

Ignore The Rules: During my investigations, I encountered signs and guidelines designed to safeguard the environment. Initially, I believed they were just ideas. However, I immediately learned that these regulations exist for a reason. For example, while visiting Grand Canyon National Park, I came across sections marked as "off-limits." Ignoring these boundaries not only endangers ecosystems, but it may also cause irrevocable damage to natural beauties.

What To Do

Educate Yourself: Before embarking on an adventure, it's important to educate yourself about the places you'll be seeing. Understanding the native flora and wildlife, as well as the specialized ecosystems, really enhanced my experiences. For example, knowing about the Sonoran Desert's distinctive plants and creatures deepened my appreciation for their responsibilities in the environment. I frequently carry field guides or use apps to identify species, which strengthens my connection to the earth.

Follow Established Trails: Follow established paths, especially in delicate situations. This not only protects native flora, but also reduces erosion. While hiking in Oak Creek Canyon, I marveled at the beauty surrounding me, feeling a sense of awe as I followed the path, knowing that I was helping to maintain the natural habitat.

Water Conservation

As someone who has traveled through Arizona's arid landscapes, I understand how valuable water is in this state. It is a resource that allows life to thrive in the desert, but it is frequently overlooked.

What Not To Do

Waste Water: During a camping trip near Lake Havasu, I observed numerous campers leaving taps running and carelessly throwing leftover water. In an area prone to droughts, such squandering is not just foolish, but also harmful. Water is essential in this location, and wasting it jeopardizes the environment's sustainability.

Pollute Water Sources: I witnessed a group at a popular swimming location in the Colorado River throwing food wrappers and other debris into the river. It was upsetting to see such a magnificent resource being treated with such disdain. Pollution not only harms aquatic life, but it also has an impact on the quality of water for future generations.

What To Do

Be Water Savvy: During my trips, I conserved water wherever possible. This entailed taking shorter showers, utilizing reusable water bottles, and regularly checking for leaks. When camping, I took my own water and planned properly to avoid wasting this valuable resource.

Clean Up After Yourself: I always packed out what I packed in, leaving no trace. At renowned destinations such as Saguaro National Park, I made it a habit to have a trash bag to collect any garbage I came across. It was a simple act, but knowing I was contributing to the cleanliness of the atmosphere made it feel substantial.

Wildlife Protection

Arizona has an astonishing variety of fauna. Every species, from the stately desert tortoise to the secretive bobcat, has an impact on the ecology.

What Not To Do

Disturb Wildlife: During a stroll in Catalina State Park, I noticed a family approaching a quail nest, which disturbed wildlife. I felt obligated to interfere and caution them that approaching too closely could stress the birds and disrupt their normal behavior. Wildlife requires space, and infringing on their domain can have devastating effects.

Feeding Wildlife: I witnessed visitors feeding squirrels and birds in parks. I discovered that this might develop to a reliance on human food, which is frequently unhealthy for animals. Feeding wildlife alters their natural foraging instincts and can change their behavior, leaving them vulnerable.

What To Do

Observe Wildlife From A Respectful Distance: Use binoculars or a zoom lens to capture moments without intruding on their space. When I noticed a herd of bighorn sheep on the cliffs of Salt River Canyon, I calmly stayed back and observed their activity, happy for the opportunity to see them in their natural habitat without interfering with their life.

Report Wildlife Sightings: I learnt to report sick or injured animals to local wildlife authorities. In one case, I noticed a terrified hawk on the side of the road near Tonto National Forest and phoned wildlife rescue. This tiny act helped me feel more connected to the local conservation initiatives.

Fire Safety

Wildfires represent a huge threat to Arizona's natural beauty and wildlife in an area that is frequently scorched by the sun. My experiences taught me the importance of fire safety.

What Not To Do

Ignore Fire Restrictions: During my travels, I observed campers setting fires in locations with fire restrictions. Ignoring these limits can result in catastrophic wildfires that destroy wildlife habitats and human communities alike. I remember feeling a sense of urgency when I reported a campfire to rangers while hiking in Coconino National Forest, knowing that my actions could help prevent a calamity.

Leave Fires Unattended: Campers should not leave flames unattended, as this can be dangerous. I was trekking in Kaibab National Forest when I came across an unattended campfire. I drenched it with water, realizing the threat that negligence represented to the ecosystem.

What To Do

Follow Guidelines: Before starting a campfire, always check municipal standards for fire regulations. If a fire was permitted, I made certain to build it in approved places, away from dry brush and flammable items. Understanding the potential threats increased my awareness of my surroundings.

Extinguish Fires Completely: After camping trips, I make sure to fully extinguish the fire. I'd sprinkle water on the ashes until they were cool to the touch. Leaving a clean campsite is crucial, and properly extinguishing flames protects the environment for future generations.

Sustainable Practices

Embracing sustainable practices has become an important aspect of my travels through Arizona. It allows me to appreciate the state's beauty while protecting it for future generations.

What Not To Do

Use Single-Use Plastics: I used to carry single-use plastic bottles and bags without thinking twice. However, I eventually learnt about the destructive impact of plastic garbage on the environment. I watched litter's impact on Arizona's landscapes, from Antelope Canyon to the Sonoran Desert.

Neglect Recycling Options: I used to overlook recycling containers in parks, preferring convenience over sustainability. I quickly realized that failing to recycle adds to landfill waste, which affects the environment.

What To Do

Opt For Reusable Alternatives: I made a conscious effort to include reusable items such as water bottles and shopping bags. This little change dramatically decreased my waste and enabled me to travel more responsibly. I discovered that utilizing a collapsible water bottle simplified my hikes while still being environmentally friendly.

Utilize Recycling Facilities: I researched recycling facilities in the areas I visited. Knowing where to properly dispose of recyclables became part of my trip routine. I recall visiting a little hamlet near Sierra Vista and discovering a local recycling program that enabled me to positively impact the environment.

Conclusion: Traveling through Arizona has helped me understand the difficult balance between curiosity and conservation. Protecting this wonderful environment is more than a responsibility; it is a pledge to preserve the beauty and richness that have captured me. Understanding ecosystems, preserving water, safeguarding wildlife, practicing fire safety, and implementing sustainable practices have helped me navigate this amazing landscape with purpose.

As you explore Arizona's stunning landscapes, I invite you to keep this awareness with you. Our choices as travelers can have a long-term influence on the environment. Each act of conservation, no matter how tiny, helps to preserve Arizona's natural beauty. Let us appreciate and maintain this area, ensuring that its beauty is preserved for future generations. Together, we can leave a legacy of stewardship and respect, allowing future visitors to enjoy the wonders of Arizona just as we did.

CHAPTER 23

DINING DO'S AND DON'TS

What To Do And Not To Do In Arizona's Culinary Scene

When I initially arrived in Arizona, I had no clue the food culture would be as colorful and varied as the surroundings. From the busy streets of Phoenix to the rural appeal of Tucson, Arizona's food culture is a beautiful tapestry woven from Native American, Mexican, and Western influences. As I explored this diverse culinary landscape, I discovered certain important dining dos and don'ts that not only improved my experience but also demonstrated respect for the local culture. Join me on this gastronomic trip as I share my observations and suggestions for experiencing the finest that Arizona has to offer.

Embracing Local Flavors

One of the first things I learned on my culinary experiences in Arizona was the value of embracing native flavors. The state's distinct culinary identity is built in its cultural diversity, and I immediately understood that delving into this aspect of dining may result in some amazing experiences.

What Not To Do

Avoid Tourist Traps: On my first day in Phoenix, I made the error of eating at a prominent tourist trap due to flashy signage and positive reviews. The cuisine was boring, and the setting lacked realism. I learnt the hard way that the highly recommended restaurants aren't always the best representations of local cuisine. It's easy to get caught up in the hoopla, but believe me when I say that going off the usual path frequently leads to hidden gems.

Disregard Cultural Significance: I observed that many travelers were unaware of the cultural significance of specific foods. When I experienced Sonoran hot dogs for the first time, I realized they are more than just a meal; they are a beloved local custom. I made a point of asking locals about the history of the meals I ordered, which only increased my appreciation for the flavors.

What To Do

Seek Out Local Eateries: My favorite meals were generally from small, family-run restaurants. One evening, I wandered onto El Charro Café in Tucson, where the walls were covered with family photos and vibrant artwork. The shredded beef enchiladas were a revelation. They possessed a richness of flavor that reflected generations of culinary heritage. Supporting local restaurants is about more than simply the cuisine; it's about connecting with your neighborhood.

Experiment With Regional Ingredients: Experiment with Arizona's local ingredients, like chili peppers and cacti. I made it a point to test dishes with these distinctive ingredients. At a farm-to-table restaurant in Sedona, I enjoyed a dish with prickly pear puree that imparted a wonderful sweetness to grilled chicken. Exploring regional flavors broadened my palate and introduced me to the richness of Arizona's culinary scene.

Understanding Etiquette

Dining etiquette varies tremendously depending on where you are. I discovered that understanding the local eating culture improves not just my meals but also my interactions with the staff and other customers.

What Not To Do

Be Rude To Servers: Some diners treated servers dismissively, as if they were only functionaries rather than integral aspects of the eating experience. I believe that respect goes a long way, particularly in the hospitality industry. Waitstaff frequently added value to my meals by sharing menu insights or suggesting pairings. I made a point of thanking everyone for their advice, which led to some delightful discoveries.

Forget To Be Patient: Don't forget to be patient when dining at popular restaurants, especially during peak hours. I noticed some diners become antsy, which produced an uncomfortable atmosphere. Instead of being frustrated, I learnt to accept the experience. While waiting at Pizzeria Bianco in Phoenix, I struck up talks with other customers, which added to the excitement of my lunch.

What To Do

Engage With Staff: When dining at The Mission in Scottsdale, I talked with the waitress to discuss the cuisine. Their recommendations, such as the pig belly tacos, proved to be a highlight of my trip. I realized that the staff often had a plethora of information about the meals and ingredients, which improved my eating experience.

Be Respectful Of Local Customs: I learnt to respect local norms, especially in locations with Native American ancestry. When dining at a restaurant that serves traditional Native American cuisine, I took the time to learn about the ingredients and cooking methods, which increased my enjoyment for the dish. It's a tribute to the culture that shaped Arizona's culinary industry.

Exploring Food Festivals

Arizona hosts a variety of food events that celebrate its culinary diversity. Attending these events became a highlight of my culinary journey, and I learned some significant things in the process.

What Not To Do

Skip The Sampling: Avoid sampling during the Tucson Culinary Festival due to the overwhelming number of food booths. My instinct was to select one or two booths and stick with them. However, I quickly understood that skipping out on trying other cuisines was a mistake. I learnt to appreciate the ability to sample tiny servings from numerous vendors, which allowed me to try a wider variety of flavors.

Rush Through The Experience: Attendees rushed through the experience, eager to taste everything at each station. I originally fell into this trap, but I quickly determined to slow down and enjoy each bite. By taking the time to savor my food and the atmosphere, I discovered that I appreciated the ingenuity that went into each dish.

What To Do

Ask Questions: Asking questions to chefs and sellers at festivals was a great experience for me. At the Arizona Taco Festival, I asked a taco seller about the secret components in their homemade salsa. The talk not only improved my understanding of the food, but also made me appreciate the craftsmanship that went into each dish.

Participate In Cooking Demos: I avidly attended cooking demonstrations at food festivals. Observing local chefs create traditional foods was eye-opening. I learned great suggestions and strategies that I later applied in my own cooking. Participating in these events also helped me connect with the culinary community, which increased my respect for Arizona's food culture.

Exploring Ethnic Cuisine

Arizona's culinary scene is a melting pot of flavors and traditions, and I quickly learnt to enjoy the numerous ethnic options. There is a variety of cuisines to try, including Mexican, Native American, and Asian.

What Not To Do

Limit Yourself To One Cuisine: During my first few days in Arizona, I focused completely on Mexican food, believing it was the state's best. While I appreciated the enchiladas and tamales, I quickly learned that limiting myself meant missing out on other delicious flavors. I learnt to appreciate the variety of ethnic foods offered in Arizona.

Assume All Mexican Food Is the Same: I mistakenly assumed that all Mexican restaurants serve the same food. When I ate at Tacos Atoyac in Phoenix, I realized the depth of Oaxacan food. The mole I had was unlike anything I'd had before, with layers of flavor that transported me to another world.

What To Do

Seek Out Authentic Ethnic Restaurants: I researched true ethnic places and had fantastic dinners. Pueblo Vida Brewing Co. in Tucson introduced me to their unique take on traditional cuisine. I enjoyed the cactus fries, which were a delicious combination of crunch and taste. These encounters taught me that each ethnic dish has a distinct tale, and exploring them introduced me to new flavors.

Try Traditional Dishes: When exploring ethnic cuisines, I recommend trying traditional dishes. At a local Indian restaurant, I had the opportunity to eat biryani and butter chicken prepared using age-old family recipes. Each taste was a celebration of the food's cultural and traditional roots.

Experience Wine And Spirits

Arizona's wine and craft beverage culture has grown in recent years, adding another dimension to the state's culinary tapestry. I made it a point to visit local vineyards and breweries on my trip.

What Not To Do

Dismiss Arizona Wines: I initially had low expectations for Arizona's wine scene. I assumed it couldn't compete against more established regions. When I toured the Willcox Wine Trail, I was pleasantly impressed by the wines' quality and range. I recognized that discounting Arizona's wine was a mistake, so I made it a point to sample several varietals during my trips.

Overlook Local Breweries: I almost missed out on Arizona's growing craft beer market while focusing on local wineries. I explored new flavors at breweries like as Mother Bunch Brewing in Phoenix, where I enjoyed a crisp citrus IPA that went well with spicy foods.

What To Do

Participate In Tastings: At Arizona Stronghold Vineyards in Cottonwood, I took part in a guided wine tasting. The experience not only exposed me to distinctive local wines, but also taught me about the winemaking process. I discovered that asking questions during tastings sometimes resulted in enlightening talks with the staff.

Pair Foods With Local Beverages: I learnt to pair my meals with local wines and beers. At Tonto Natural Bridge State Park, I brought a picnic with local cheeses and a bottle of Arizona wine. This attention to detail elevated an average meal into a memorable one.

Conclusion: Dining in Arizona has become one of the highlights of my travels, providing an opportunity to connect with the local culture while also sampling a variety of delicacies. By embracing local cuisines, adhering to dining etiquette, attending food festivals, and delving into ethnic offers, I discovered a culinary world as diverse as the state itself.

As I relished each meal, I became more appreciative of the stories behind the food, the people who cook them, and the ethnicities that contribute to Arizona's rich culinary scene. Every taste contains a connection to the land, the people, and a legacy of flavors waiting to be discovered. So, the next time you're in Arizona, remember these dos and don'ts and set out on a culinary excursion that will leave your taste buds dancing and your heart satisfied. Bon appétit!

CHAPTER 24

DEPARTURE TIPS

What To Remember Before Leaving Arizona

As my time in Arizona came to an end, I found myself pondering on all of the experiences and memories I had made during my travels. From the sun-kissed desert scenery to the vibrant cities filled with culture, this state has provided me with an adventure unlike any other. However, as any seasoned traveler knows, leaving a location is equally vital as arriving. Here are my departing advice, a collection of lessons learnt and observations obtained from my tour through this stunning desert state.

Take Time For Reflection

One of the most fulfilling elements of travel is the chance to reflect on your experiences. As I prepared to depart Arizona, I made a point of pausing to reflect on everything I had experienced.

What Not To Do

Rush The Departure: I used to rush my departures, focused entirely on logistics and ignoring the emotional impact of leaving a location. During my journey to Arizona, I realized the importance of slowing down. One afternoon, I found a peaceful location at Tempe Town Lake and sat on a seat viewing the water, the sun shining golden rays across the surface. As I watched the sun set, I felt overwhelmed with appreciation for the experiences I'd had. I realized how vital it is to take a minute to breathe and appreciate everything this place has offered me before leaving.

Forget To Capture Memories: I once left a trip without fully documenting my best experiences, leaving me feeling like I missed something important. This time, I made an effort to take photos, write notes in my trip diary, and even collect tiny mementos from the sites I visited. Whether it was a postcard from Sedona or a dish from a local restaurant, these mementos of my trip would serve as treasured memories of my time in Arizona.

What To Do

Journal Your Thoughts: I started writing about my day every evening. This practice enabled me to process my experiences and feelings. On one particular night, while I scribbled my thoughts about trekking the Bright Angel Trail at the Grand Canyon, I remembered the thrill of reaching the viewpoint and the breathtaking scenery that surrounding me. Journaling became a technique to preserve those feelings and ensure that they did not fade away with time.

Engage With Locals: As my leaving date approached, I looked out ways to interact with the locals one more time. I went to a café in Flagstaff and began up a chat with the barista, who told me about her favorite hiking areas. These interactions broadened my awareness of the culture and gave me a sense of belonging that I would keep with me.

Souvenirs And Mementos

Before departing Arizona, I felt obliged to take home a bit of the state. But I wanted to chose my keepsakes carefully, ensuring that they reflected my experiences rather than simply filling my baggage.

What Not To Do

Buy Generic Souvenirs: I used to buy generic mementos like fridge magnets and keychains that lacked personal value. In Arizona, I was keen to find unique objects that expressed the soul of my adventure. At a Tucson artisan market, I discovered handmade jewelry created from native stones. Each object had a narrative, and I found myself gravitating toward items that spoke to my experiences.

Neglect Local Artisans: I made sure not to ignore local artisans. I went to a pottery factory in Sedona and witnessed the craftsmen shape clay into stunning works of art. Buying a handcrafted vase not only helped the local economy, but it also reminded me of the creativity and talent that exists in this state.

What To Do

Choose Meaningful Souvenirs: I chose trinkets with personal importance. A bottle of locally made prickly pear syrup reminded me of my excursions in the Sonoran Desert, where I tried the fruit for the first time. I also carried back a book of Native American legends that I had purchased at a local bookshop, a wealth of cultural knowledge that would keep the spirit of Arizona alive long after I had left.

Document The Tales Behind Your Souvenirs: I made a point of noting each thing I purchased. When I got home, I'd gaze at the vase from Sedona and remember the pottery studio's warm, friendly atmosphere and the chats I had with the artisans. These stories would add layers of significance to my souvenirs.

Stay Connected

Leaving a place does not imply cutting ties. Staying connected in today's digital world is easier than ever, and I wanted to keep the contacts I had built throughout my travels in Arizona.

What Not To Do

Ignore Social Media Opportunities: I had previously underestimated the importance of social media in keeping friendships. I discovered that sharing my experiences through images and posts might foster a sense of community among other tourists and locals. I'd met some wonderful people in various places, and failing to connect with them online would mean losing contact with those important relationships.

Neglect Local Groups And Pages: I neglected to follow local groups and pages about Arizona's culture and activities. This time, I made a concentrated effort to join internet forums and social media groups devoted to Arizona. It created opportunities for continued connection with the local community, even from afar.

What To Do

Follow Locals On Social Media: After meeting great people in Arizona, I followed them on social media. This allowed me to stay up to date on their lives as well as state events. I appreciated viewing photographs of beautiful sunsets over the Grand Canyon and new restaurants in Phoenix. Despite being hundreds of miles away, I felt like I was still a part of the Arizona community.

Share My Experiences: I used social media to share my trip adventures in Arizona, including images and anecdotes. I was pleasantly pleased by the interest from friends and fans who wanted to hear about my trip. Sharing my experiences inspired others to discover Arizona's splendor.

Final Exploration

Before departing, I took one last look at the sites that had captured my heart. This practice helped me say goodbye in a meaningful way.

What Not To Do

Skip The Last Visit To Favorites: In prior trips, I would rush to the airport without revisiting my favorite spots. This time, I made it a point to spend my final day in Sedona exploring the breathtaking red rock formations that had left me in awe. Standing at Cathedral Rock, I took a moment to enjoy the scenery, feeling a sensation of calm sweep over me. Each visit became a farewell, a way to commemorate the beauty I had witnessed.

Don't Limit Your Exploration: Instead than focusing on popular attractions, consider exploring off the beaten path. However, I discovered that some of the most spectacular moments occur when you deviate from the expected path. On a whim, I went to a lesser-known hiking trail near Prescott, where I discovered a peaceful lake surrounded by pines. It became a secret jewel in my memory, the ideal final investigation.

What To Do

Plan A Farewell Day: I used my last day in Arizona to visit my favorite spots. I returned to Phoenix's Desert Botanical Garden and enjoyed a leisurely stroll among the cacti and wildflowers. Each flower seemed like the desert's final hug. It was a wonderful way to reflect on my adventure and savor my final minutes in this great state.

In my final hours, I sought a peaceful location in Saguaro National Park and meditated. I closed my eyes, took long breaths, and thanked Arizona for everything she had given me. I placed a modest token—a stone I had collected during my travels—on a ledge as a symbolic gesture of leaving a bit of my heart in this beautiful area.

Preparing For The Journey Home

As I packed my things, I made sure to be ready for the voyage ahead. Leaving Arizona was bittersweet, but I was delighted to bring a piece of it back with me.

What Not To Do

Overpack And Stress: Overpacking can cause unnecessary stress at airports. This time, I made an attempt to pack lightly.

I carefully selected my favorite attire and souvenirs to avoid carrying too much baggage. Travel should be liberating, not stressful.

Forget Important Documents: I once forgot vital travel documents while hastily leaving. This time, I made a checklist to verify that I had everything I needed: my passport, tickets, and any reservations for my next journey.

What To Do

Organize My Souvenirs: To organize my keepsakes, I carefully wrapped fragile objects and saved room in my suitcase for particular mementos. Each piece represented a narrative, and I wanted to make sure they arrived home safely.

Stay Hydrated: To prepare for my journey in Arizona's dry climate, I prioritized staying hydrated. Before traveling to the airport, I drank some water and had a wonderful prickly pear lemonade at a café, which made me feel revived and ready to embark on my next journey.

Conclusion: As I said goodbye to Arizona, I took with me not only memories but also vital lessons that would define my future adventures. Taking the time to ponder, selecting meaningful souvenirs, remaining connected, and savoring my final adventures had enhanced my trip and ensured that my leaving was as rewarding as my arrival.

Traveling is more than just exploring new locations; it's also about making connections, embracing cultures, and leaving a piece of oneself behind. Arizona had greeted me with wide arms, and as I boarded the plane, I knew this magnificent state would always have a special place in my heart. Until next time, Arizona.

Made in the USA
Las Vegas, NV
07 March 2025

900e4d7e-7aef-45c4-88b1-b3211427ecc3R01